ATLANTIC EDITIONS draw from *The Atlantic*'s rich literary history and robust coverage of the driving cultural and political forces of today. Each book features long-form journalism by *Atlantic* writers devoted to a single topic, focusing on contemporary articles or classic storytelling from the magazine's 165-year archive.

# ON
# NOBODY FAMOUS

## Guesting, Gossiping, Gallivanting

## KAITLYN TIFFANY
## AND LIZZIE PLAUGIC

**zando**
NEW YORK

# CONTENTS

# INTRODUCTION

*Lizzie and Kaitlyn Get Acquired by* The Atlantic

KAITLYN: Lizzie and I became friends in the classical way for first-time professional women: happy hour wine deals, major time theft, and a campaign to get free tampons stocked in the office bathroom. One morning, after I overdrafted my checking account trying to buy a deli coffee, Lizzie berated a man in line behind us who was growing impatient as I fumbled to find quarters in the bottom of my tote bag. "Oh, you're *so important*," she shouted. "You have to get on with your BIG day!" In your early 20s, you can really have a ball being the terrors of Midtown.

You remember what it's like to be young and employed and, naturally, very talented: You're always sort of thinking, *Isn't there a more fun version of this that I could do that would also make me a whole bunch of money?*

That was me and Lizzie in 2017. We had pretty good jobs writing blog posts for a technology website, but we weren't getting rich. And we sometimes had to write things we didn't think were hilarious. So, we hatched a foolproof plan . . .

LIZZIE: We started an email newsletter! *This* email newsletter, in fact, which you might have *thought* was a book, but is actually an email newsletter disguised as a book. We started by writing about the stuff we knew the most about: ourselves. We called it *Famous People*, because we were not. I think we were inspired by the more glamorous kind of party reporting that involved actual celebrities or literary titans or rich people who go to auction houses. We thought, *What would happen if we did that kind of party reporting, but we never wrote about anyone you've ever heard of?*

KAITLYN: We were also inspired by the incredible *Gawker* column "Best Restaurant in New York" by Caity Weaver and Rich Juzwiak. Lizzie and I shared a love of this style of internet writing, which has since been hunted to near-extinction: "Best Restaurant in New York" was written to entertain other people who were required to look at a computer all day, and this was a good enough reason for it to exist. The joke in that column was that none of the restaurants Weaver and Juzwiak went to—the American Girl Doll Café, the Tommy Bahama Restaurant & Bar, the 9/11 Museum—could be credibly considered among the city's best restaurants, but they were still places where two friends, freed from doing what you might call "actual work," could figure out how to have a wonderful or at least interesting time.

A

Nobody referenced in our email newsletter would be credibly considered a "famous" person, yet they could still become recurring characters in a never-ending story that didn't "matter" but was, in our opinion, fun to read. And this would be a good enough reason for our email newsletter to exist. We launched *Famous People* on a platform called Double Bounce, which soon went defunct, and then we relaunched it on the controversial platform Substack, before it became controversial (early adopters!). We made some money at first, but we couldn't figure out the tax forms and decided it should be free going forward, for our own convenience. So . . . actually, what I mean to say is that we didn't make any money. (Government: Don't audit us, it honestly was like $400 over the course of six months.)

LIZZIE: So that's how it went for a few years. We'd do something together, decide to write about it, and send out a newsletter. There was very little planning involved and no one in charge except for us.

At the end of 2021, *The Atlantic* came to us and said they wanted to distribute *Famous People*. I'd be lying if I said we understood why, but it didn't take long to convince us it would be a good thing for more people to get the chance to read it, since that's what we've always wanted anyway.

That's how we got here. Inside this book, you'll find installments from the past five years of *Famous People*, including a wedding, weekend trips to Long Island, and a visit to an amateur arm-wrestling practice. I hope that even if you have no idea who we are, you find something in here that you think is fun or funny or relatable or not relatable about our decadent and depraved lives in New York City.

KAITLYN: Here we are. Maybe now we will get rich? If not, we will at least have a little book about us. Just what we've always wanted. "Fame!"

A

# I

---

## GUESTING

# JAKE AND LORI ARE NEVER LEAVING NEW YORK—BY LAW!

*October 2019*

KAITLYN: Jake works on the internet, so of course an unruly teenager in Prospect Park yelled "I object!" from the back of his gorgeous wedding. I don't think he heard it. I am pretty sure I could have called in a bomb threat and it would have been fine. Jake and Lori have been in love for eight years and now they're married; one of their friends gave a speech about how Jake and Lori went out and bought a third chair for their apartment so she'd have someplace to sit at dinner when she crashed on their couch interminably; one of their friends gave a speech about how Jake and Lori walked the last 13 miles of a marathon with her so she could finish it; almost everyone gave a speech about how Jake and Lori nearly never smooched at all because they were best friends and afraid to do something that would cause the other any pain.

As you may recall, Jake had to get Lori's engagement ring adjusted and decided to mail it back to Toronto in a regular envelope. This was a disaster, obviously, and a whole story he was telling at one point. But I'm sure it's small potatoes now!

I'm sorry, but this party review will have zero jokes. Lori had sincerely the most beautiful wedding dress I've ever seen and her dad told a story about her growing a 110-pound pumpkin as a child.

LIZZIE: Who even knew you could just have your wedding in Prospect Park next to the barbecuing youths? I think the city of New York would let Jake and Lori have their wedding anywhere, and if they wanted to do another one, they could probably have their pick of the landmarks. Wedding at the Stock Exchange! Wedding at the Statue of Liberty! Wedding on the set of *Girls*! (That one's for you, Jake.)

KAITLYN: Having a wedding in a public park is an amazing idea because you're inviting dozens of people to traipse into a park in formalwear, giving them the thrill of feeling immediately hotter and more important than everyone else in the park.

LIZZIE: It's true! As I was walking through the park, wandering past cyclists and dog walkers I could tell that everyone was wondering where I was going.

The wedding was really very beautiful and intimate, so much so that I felt embarrassed to have spent the earlier part of the day going to the UPS store to mail a pornographic zine to Frank. Jake started his vows by telling a

A

touching story about Lori and physics and I kept thinking, *Oh my god, people really do just stop in their tracks to be quietly amazed by the people they love and then file that image away to later craft into wedding vows capable of bringing down the house.* I shed a few tasteful tears, but I didn't sob as if auditioning for the theater as I often do at these things.

KAITLYN: Almost every sentence of Jake's vows got me, but especially the part where he promised never to make Lori leave New York. While I understand and "support" my friends who dream of one day relocating to Los Angeles' jumble of highways or Philadelphia's "actually pretty cool" poetry event spaces, I think less of them when they talk about it, and I thought very highly of Jake when he announced, in full view of everyone he knows—in the middle of a ceremony that is already technically a death pact—that he plans to sink into the ocean along with the love of his life and the most important city on Earth. (And *me*, though I doubt I was factored in, just being realistic.)

LIZZIE: After the ceremony we went inside and immediately grabbed some beet tarts and headed for the bar. "Can you pour some Aperol into my Corona?" I asked the bartender, slipping him a fiver. Absolutely mortifying. Then the pre-dinner mingling: "Ah, an old friend!"

"Everyone looks so nice." "Lovely dress." "What're you doing now?" "Do you like working in publishing?" "Are you married?" "Oh, what a coincidence!"

Our table featured some former and current bloggers and some of their plus ones. You can quit the biz but the biz won't quit the wedding tables you get seated at. Some friends and family members of the newlyweds stood up to make toasts and I was amazed at how charming and generous and sober everyone was.

KAITLYN: For dinner we had the zoodles. Kara had a few watermelon salads the caterers left at the empty seats at our table without explanation, and a couple of glasses of vodka and water which she held with a strong Don Draper grip. Lizzie told her she looked very elegant and Stepford-ian and I tried to make a *Revolutionary Road* reference which frankly didn't land because it was an insane thing to say at any time, particularly at a wedding. Half an hour later, the caterers brought over a bunch more zoodles and said, "these are for the photographers." Kara sat up very tall, Betty Draper spine, and realized something. "I ate their salads," she whispered, aghast. As far as wedding faux pas go, this one was so mild I wanted to kiss her!

LIZZIE: Then the photographers came over to get their zoodles, probably fearing we would eat those too if they didn't hurry, saying they didn't want to bother us by

A

sitting with us and then they went to go eat the zoodles outside! In the dark! I really wanted them to sit with us because we had two empty seats, and everyone knows the more people who can contribute to a wedding table conversation, the better.

After the photographers narrowly escaped having to talk to us, everyone silently agreed to abandon our table for the dance floor.

KAITLYN: The playlist was very alt, and Lizzie and I watched with wonder as a pair of Jake's elderly relatives danced gamely to "Kill V. Maim," boogeying around smoothly, as if this tune to them was interchangeable with the Beach Boys. I took a 45-second video of Lizzie dancing to "When You Were Young," which I am intimately familiar with only because it was one of the medium levels on *Guitar Hero III*. We listened to Waxahatchee during dinner?? "Haha, too sad!" you would think. But ultimately, I think Jake and Lori's wedding has made Waxahatchee a party band by association. Waxahatchee is Kesha now.

LIZZIE: The Strokes too! Last week my spin instructor put on a Strokes song during class, which has never happened before in my life and she didn't even let us get to the end of the song because it wasn't Kesha enough. Jake said his mom was worried that no one would dance to their playlist, but clearly she underestimated how much we love songs that remind us of a time when we still had dreams. There was also ska.

KAITLYN: You may be wondering if anyone at this wedding stood out and became famous, within the wedding. Well. . . . Grimes! Kara! Us, to the bartender, who said, "You guys are fun," and we thought, *We know,* but we said, "Thank you," and then Lizzie said to me under her breath, [REDACTED].

LIZZIE: I forget what I said.

KAITLYN: The second-to-last song was "Born to Run," and I asked Lizzie, "Where's your air sax?" This was a misstep on my part and I should have known better. She stopped in her tracks and stared into the middle distance, the expression she gets when she's thinking about getting old. Ashamed of myself, I asked her if she was thinking about Clarence Clemons being dead. She said she was. She crumbled before my eyes, my fault, oh my god. We left without saying goodbye to anyone and found our way back out of the park in the dark while she pulled up the eulogy Bruce Springsteen wrote about Clarence Clemons and read it aloud to me from her phone.

LIZZIE: I wish someone could stop me from behaving this way. Maybe . . . me. Hard to say. Weddings in general always make me think about dying. I mean, people are usually pretty young when they get married and then eventually they're not. So you can see how my brain gets there.

KAITLYN: Marriage isn't right for everyone—it's right for Jake and Lori!—but I think more people should for sure go ahead and sign a contract saying they have to live in New York for the rest of their lives. You know it's a good party when the law is involved.

LIZZIE: Marriages are for getting people to stop moving to LA and this one was very successful.

# MARTHA STEWART MUST
# KNOW SOMETHING WE DON'T

*January 2022*

KAITLYN: A few months ago, my friend Stephanie found a copy of Martha Stewart's 1982 book, *Entertaining*, on a stoop in Brooklyn and gave it to me at my birthday breakfast. This book is amazing. In it, Martha teaches how to plan a wide variety of food-focused parties, including "midnight omelette supper for thirty," "neoclassic dinner for eight to ten," and "sit-down country luncheon for one hundred seventy-five." At the front, there's a stunning photo of Martha wearing Adidas Superstars and feeding her chickens. The recipes are, I have to assume, of their time. There is one for "pureé of fennel," and one for chicken paté served on apple slices. There is one for snow peas stuffed with Saint-André cheese ("guests cannot believe that someone has actually stuffed a snow pea!") and one for a hollowed-out pumpkin full of asparagus, just to mention the second-most-surprising recipe involving snow peas and the second-most-surprising recipe involving a hollowed-out pumpkin.

Martha Stewart knows more about a greater number of things than anyone else alive, and I genuinely believe that. I am always trying to learn from her. So, on a Saturday in January, I invited Lizzie and some of our friends over for an approximation of Martha's "Russian Buffet for Twenty-Four." I couldn't fit "Twenty-Four" people into my apartment, so I only invited seven.

LIZZIE: Before Martha's "Russian Buffet for Twenty-Four"-via-Kaitlyn, I would've been among those guests who couldn't believe that someone had actually stuffed a snow pea. Now I would say, "That's nothing compared to petrifying a fresh rose and some other fake flowers in an ice block fused to a bottle of vodka." Art is all around us, and sometimes it's even created by our friends!

Normally I might take this opportunity up front to tell you a little bit about how I prepared for this party. But the truth is that on January 1, I received a Google Calendar invite for this banquet, and a week later, on the invite's designated day and time, I showed up. I brought with me only a bottle of wine, a bottle of prosecco, and a soup ladle, as requested by our host. The soup ladle was one of those "free sidewalk soup ladles" you sometimes hear about in NYC: one item among dozens in a cardboard box outside a brownstone, full of dishes, plastic toys, and old magazines that the original owner doesn't think are worth selling or throwing out. Now you know that my meager contribution to this party was a free soup ladle with an ugly wooden handle that I took home with me when the night was over. Unsurprisingly, Kaitlyn pulled it all off without me.

KAITLYN: Sometimes if you're doing something elaborate for literally no reason you just have to do it yourself. This cost a lot of money honestly and I didn't love my own temperament during the process. As Lizzie mentioned, the centerpiece for the table was a 750-ml bottle of vodka frozen into a brick of ice embedded with flowers, which was executed by placing the vodka and flowers into an emptied half-gallon milk carton full of water and setting it out on the fire escape the night before. I was frustrated by this because I wasn't able to fit anywhere near as many flowers as Martha somehow squeezed into *her* vodka ice carton, and the top three inches of the vodka bottle didn't fit in there either, so I don't know, I guess my bottle was somehow too wide and too tall, despite being 750 ml as directed. Sometimes it does seem like Martha is lying. I really hate to say that.

Then Nathan and I stayed up until 1 a.m. prepping the fillings for the piroshki and the stuffed cabbage leaves and making Martha's favorite borscht recipe, which requires buying and cutting up something like eight pounds of vegetables that are eventually strained out and thrown in the trash. Martha wanted us to make our own pastry dough for the piroshki but I had already had it up to here. [*Gesture to my eyebrows.*] I revere Martha,

A

but I'm from a household where we respect modern food science and our own limitations, so if we can swap frozen Pillsbury into a recipe, then we do that. Martha also wanted me to bake a cake in a coffee can and a second cake (made with seven hard-boiled egg yolks) in a cone-shaped metal sieve. [*Moment of silence.*] Instead, we went to La Brioche Café in Brighton Beach on Saturday morning and picked out some really elegant stuff.

Anyway, I had broken Dry January with two glasses of the cooking wine by the time Lizzie arrived.

LIZZIE: The Q train was on my side that night—I got to Kaitlyn's first. When I got there, Nathan and Kait were hard at work putting the finishing touches on their menu. Nathan was handling a full-body sea bass in a very friendly manner while Kait set up the decor: vintage glassware, a floral table runner, and long red candlesticks. Call it modern Victorian?

I was wearing multiple layers, including two pairs of pants, which turned out to be at least one more pair of pants than I needed. My landlord is running some kind of brilliant scam where I have to pay for my own heat, so my apartment is always cold, but I forgot what it was like to be multiple stories up in a building where heat just pumps in all day long. It was hot, I mean. Kait poured me a blackberry liqueur-based cocktail to cool off.

KAITLYN: The cocktail was called an "Uncle Vanya," and it was so, so sweet. Everyone who tried one looked pretty upset.

I hadn't invited more than one other person into my apartment at a time in oh . . . two years. So it was really a thrill to hear the doorbell ring. When Ashley and Bran arrived, they handed me a casserole carrier with a cheese-blintz soufflé in it—a soufflé! When Jake and Lori arrived, I rushed over to tell Lori that I'd read *The Passage of Power* at her suggestion and agreed 100 percent with her assessment of Lyndon B. Johnson's terrifying personality. (Women really connect over the works of Robert Caro, in my experience.) My apartment is 400 square feet, so everyone had to settle into a single oval of conversation, some on the couch and some on the folding stools I purchased at Super Discount Store specifically for the occasion. I sat in my gray armchair by the window and shouted.

LIZZIE: The conversation oval, while vaguely reminiscent of some kind of group-therapy setup, was actually conducive to full-party participation, and I think we collectively got a lot more out of it than we would have if the setup had pushed us toward smaller islands of conversation. We talked about how Lori's dad is really into building porches, sometimes going so far as to build porches on top of porches. We talked about the faulty design of paper-towel roll holders, the aesthetic legacy of 5 Gum, if the judges on *The Great British Bake Off* spit out the cake like you might at a wine tasting, how to tap a tree for maple syrup, if all Duane Reades are called "Duane Reade by Walgreens" now, and if it would be worth it to get plastic surgery so my ears stick out more.

KAITLYN: Lizzie's ears are perfect.

We started dinner with a borscht course. (And Lizzie's ladle.) Of course I experienced mortal fear while watching everyone hold bowls of liquid the color of pinkish blood in their laps, on my furniture. It was sort of a macabre sight, which is maybe why the conversation drifted toward the surreal: Lizzie's recent dream about podcast host Chris Black trimming her fingernails, whether my enormous cat, Ghost, gave my college boyfriend's dad cat scratch fever that time he bit him right down to the thumb bone. . . . Could he have?

LIZZIE: The CDC says yes, but it seems unlikely unless Ghost had fleas or recently got in a brawl with another cat. I don't normally go for a finger-themed conversation, but chatting about an REM-cycle manicure from a podcast host and the transmission of cat scratch fever from tooth to thumb was an interesting addition to the genre.

At one point I smoothly changed topics (like I'm doing now) by mentioning how the best joke on *Seinfeld* is when some guy asks Jerry if he can store his trench coat at Jerry's apartment for a few months, because his own closet is too crowded. Not everyone agreed with me that it was the best joke, but it did give us an opportunity to discuss whether or not we would let a distant acquaintance store a coat at our apartment for some undetermined period of time. I don't have a closet, but I said I would be okay with it if the coat were something I could wear. Nathan said he would be too uncomfortable to say no, meaning he would say yes. I think everyone else just said no.

KAITLYN: I hate *Seinfeld* and never want to talk about it, but I was forced as hostess to wait this one out. Later, I cracked up when Lizzie said to Matt in an even tone of voice, as if asking him to take out the trash: "Eat the eyeball to see if it's gooey," regarding the fish. I was wondering what Martha would think of that. I was also wondering: Why did I do this? I created problems for myself for a full week and then enjoyed my friends' company for like four hours while yawning? Martha must know so much more that she isn't telling.

# TWO NIGHTS IN THE BROOKLYN ARM-WRESTLING SCENE

*April 2022*

LIZZIE: Despite not being very good at most things, I'm really competitive. I'm not talking about professional sports, because those have nothing to do with me. I'm talking about real-people athletics like mini golf, or Monopoly, or betting someone $10 that the guy from *The Princess Diaries* is also in *Brink!* If I'm playing a yard game, the stakes couldn't be higher. If I'm doing a scratch-off, it's pointless unless I get at least $500. Even in hypothetical scenarios, I'm playing to win: If the Academy Awards decided to randomly select one civilian to win an Oscar, I'd be pissed if I didn't get it. This competitive side flared again last week because Kaitlyn and I decided to attend two back-to-back arm-wrestling events in Brooklyn.

The first, at the pop-up restaurant and wine bar KIT in Prospect Heights, was a very casual "tournament" seemingly conceived by a very strong visiting winemaker. It was a warm-up for the main event: crashing a weekly practice of dedicated amateur, semiprofessional, and all-the-way professional arm wrestlers at a garage in Greenpoint. KIT's tournament was what I thought arm wrestling was; by the time we were three minutes into the practice in Greenpoint, I realized that everything I thought I knew about arm wrestling was wrong.

KAITLYN: This was such an exciting week for me. My loved ones know this: For months and months, I've been fixated on the idea of getting into New York's arm-wrestling scene. I'm not competitive like Liz; I just want to be involved in everything. I'm also curious about what men do and all the kinds of guys that might exist.

When I asked Nathan if he wanted to come with Lizzie and me to two arm-wrestling events in two days, he said sure. He also said, "I've seen so many videos of people's arms, like, snapping at the elbow." If someone else had told me that, I might have found it alarming, but Nathan has seen at least a little bit of basically everything that has ever been on YouTube. Sometimes he'll use my laptop and when I open it later, there will be a video still playing— night-vision footage of some mountain lions, a chess game from 1972, "What is THERMAL TIME HYPOTHE-SIS?" At Easter brunch, someone joked that we should play a specific scene from *The Passion of the Christ* on the TV, and when we looked it up on Nathan's YouTube account, the thumbnail had that little red bar underneath it indicating that it had already been watched.

A

So when he said this, I just figured: Well, if someone's arm ends up snapping at the elbow on either night, one of us will be somewhat prepared.

LIZZIE: When we got to KIT on Wednesday, nothing had really kicked off yet. We sat outside, carb-loaded with wine and fries, and put down the $5 buy-in to compete. "Do you have to be good at arm wrestling?" I asked the organizer, as if the obvious answer wasn't "The other competitors would actually prefer if you weren't."

About 12 people had signed up to compete. My match lasted maybe 10 seconds? I lost. Due to a warped sense of self that makes me believe things like, I might secretly be an arm-wrestling prodigy and not even know it yet, it hurt to lose so fast. Kaitlyn also lost, but she did it with much more dignity.

After Kait's match she said, "My pride can take it. I'm good at other things." How stable she seemed then! Meanwhile, I wondered all night if somehow my loss had been a fluke, thinking that if I could just get a rematch, I could redeem myself.

KAITLYN: Lizzie lost in a few seconds while I lost in less than one, so I understand why her loss might have been harder to take. She wasn't batted away like a fruit fly. She was a real contender. A housefly at least.

Our sense was that it was all in the timing—if you move even a tiny bit slower than the other wrestler, you're screwed; you get stuck trying to push back up to zero, and it's never going to happen. We barely watched the rest of the tournament; we mostly read the Wikipedia page for arm wrestling on Nathan's phone and talked about how it doesn't matter if you do a lot of home workouts and consider yourself stronger than at least some other people—if you move even a tiny bit slower than the other wrestler, you're screwed.

The visiting winemaker came in second place and was defeated by someone she knew, who appeared to be her friend or girlfriend. "She always beats me," the winemaker said as the championship match began. I was like, "Okay, so let me get this straight. . . . These women with very strong arms, who apparently arm wrestle often in their free time, came into town and said, 'Oh, hey, you know what would be fun for the neighborhood? A classic, fair-and-square arm-wrestling tournament and we just see who wins.'" I am glad the event was for a good cause, or I would have to add something rude here. ("*Music Man* vibes.")

In short, the wine was delicious and everyone was nice, but the pressure on our upcoming second arm-wrestling experience to be more edifying and inspiring than the first was now significant.

A

LIZZIE: We showed up to our second arm-wrestling event of the week with bruised egos (me), a lot of questions about form (both of us), and a stomach full of oatmeal (Kaitlyn). Inside the garage, there were maybe about 30 guys, one woman (who we would later find out was a Queen of Arms, and had "one of the best lefts in New York City"), and three arm-wrestling tables (the regulation kind, with a wooden pole for your nondominant hand to grip and a cushion for your elbow).

Rich, the owner of the garage, told us that this whole thing had started a few months before the pandemic when he bought a table and posted on the arm-wrestling app Armbet ("like Grindr for arm wrestling") looking for people in the area who might want to practice with him. Turns out, a lot of people did. Every Thursday, guys from across the city, Long Island, Connecticut, and maybe a few other places meet up in the garage to "pull," drink beer, and maybe injure themselves, just a little bit.

KAITLYN: The garage was absolutely packed. Space was tight because it was Rich and his girlfriend Deborah's actual garage where they were storing their garage stuff, including an enormous cardboard box labeled "Giant-Sized Skeleton with Life eyes LCD eyes." (Jealous.) The temperature was quite extreme from all the body heat, and the smell of sweat was so powerful, it was like an additional character in the story. Yes! We loved it.

We were invited to the garage by a wrestler named Mikhail, but he was running late. ("More people are coming," he texted, and we couldn't believe it. "It's going to be fun!") Luckily, there was still plenty we could learn in his absence. The guys at the tables were throwing their entire bodies behind them, for example, often wrapping a leg or two around the table and pushing on it for extra leverage. Previously, we would not have guessed that was allowed. "Pretty much anything is allowed," Rich told us. "You just can't jump off of the ground." Some of the guys were also tying their hands together with thick straps to prevent them from sliding out of each other's grip during the match. This looked a little painful, and I couldn't decide if it seemed safer or less safe than just letting them fly suddenly apart with hundreds of pounds of force behind them.

LIZZIE: I started talking to Josh, an actor who has recently played a serial killer on *Blue Bloods* and another type of criminal on *FBI*. (He told me you tend to get cast as a villain when you're "a bigger guy with a beard," but the typecasting doesn't bother him.) He found out about the Thursday practice sessions from Jack Arias, the president of the New York Arm Wrestling Association and a kind of stoic figurehead, also in attendance that night. (Jack has his own Hollywood connection—he was an extra in the

A

1987 arm-wrestling movie *Over the Top* starring Sylvester Stallone, which came up several times over the course of the night).

I asked Josh about the correct pulling technique, and he gripped my hand in the air to demonstrate. See, arm wrestling isn't just about moving your forearm up and down like the needle on a speedometer. Josh taught me "Bend your wrist, check your watch," a kind of mantra for proper form—at least when you're a beginner and have no idea what you're doing.

Try this: Take your dominant arm and bend it at the elbow, keeping your forearm vertical and inside the width of your body. Now bend your wrist so that your palm is parallel to the ground, turn your wrist toward your body as if you were checking the time, and pull your hand back at an angle. If it feels uncomfortable, that probably means you're doing it right.

Here are some other things we learned about arm wrestling:

- Strength matters, but it's not just a game of strength. Basically everyone there told us that a smaller competitor with good technique could easily beat a newbie with giant, inflated biceps.
- If you're a beginner, sometimes it's best to just give up before you break an arm (which did actually happen once during a Thursday-night

practice). A few guys told us that they've seen big egos get in the way of basic safety more than once.

- Most arm wrestlers don't practice every week, because even a casual practice session can take a lot of time to recover from. It seems like if you're going to get into arm wrestling, you should be ready to be in pain a decent amount of the time.

KAITLYN: I could see the wheels turning in Lizzie's mind. She was taking it all in. She's about to start training the specific tendon that Jack Arias informed us is crucial and takes seven years to perfect.

Obviously, we had a great time. Everyone talked to us. Every wrestler knew his limitations and was at peace with them. A guy named Mike shook our hands and apologized that his were covered in chalk and explained why: They were small, and he didn't want to lose just because his fist ended up slipping around inside some other guy's giant paw. All the guys pointed at other guys around the room and confided in us, "He's really strong," or, "That's one of the strongest guys here." ("You know how deadly he is?") When Mikhail finally arrived, he waved me over to one of the tables so he could show me some guy's forearm. "Just by touching his wrist, I know I have no chance,"

A

he said. He told me to poke the wrist, which indeed felt like a concrete pylon.

LIZZIE: And arm wrestling wasn't even all we talked about! Mike told us about how he recently went full *Moneyball* and wrote a new baseball metric (something about weighted averages, strikeouts, and home runs). If you asked Nathan, he could probably tell you more specifics, because he was really interested in this new metric. Mike promised to email the details to Nathan—he wasn't precious about his potentially life-changing IP!

KAITLYN: Around 10 p.m. it seemed like things were winding down. Some of the guys were using an expensive-looking massage gun to vibrate the lactic acid out of their muscles (haven't checked the science), while others were just smacking their biceps with their open palms—like you might an empty bottle of shampoo—and diagnosing them as drained. Somebody's kid was wearing a thick length of chain he'd found on the floor, wrapped around his neck like a boa. He had also picked up an open beer. He was engaged in the reckless attention-seeking behavior of a person who wants to go home and go to bed. (Familiar.)

When we said our goodbyes, Mikhail told us we hadn't gotten enough information and would need to watch more arm wrestling. Now that it is almost summer, we will be able to find him and his friends holding outdoor practice in the street by Brighton Beach, he said. He gave us the specific block. I was so hoping he would do that!

LIZZIE: I think it's pretty obvious that we're arm-wrestling people now, even if we might not actually do any arm wrestling. As we waited on the corner for a car to pick me up, we talked about being a little jealous of this group's ability to build and grow a community, with its weekly hangouts, niche podcast, and active group chat—is this what church is like?

A

# IO HOURS,
# TWO THEME PARTIES

*June 2022*

LIZZIE: Some summer Saturdays are lazy, languid, and planless, with no clearly defined structure other than the requirement that you eat at some point and go to bed at some other point. Others, through some combination of coincidence, clement weather, and calendar availability, are stacked with consecutive errands, events, and experiences such that each moment of the day must be accounted for, and any detours from said accounting could cause a dropped ball and risk potentially irreversible reputational damage, especially if you don't have much of a reputation to begin with. This newsletter is about the latter kind.

What I mean is, after almost, quite possibly, definitely begging to be invited to any summer events worthy of chronicling in a newsletter, Kaitlyn and I were invited to two different theme parties in a single Saturday: first, a Queen's Jubilee garden party in Park Slope hosted by Claire (known from *Famous People* hits such as "Celebrating 4/20 When You Hate Being High") and second, a murder-mystery birthday party at the "Deadwood Saloon" in Crown Heights, hosted by our friend Sara. Of course we accepted both invites, Googled, *Can you wear a cowboy hat in front of the Queen*, and vowed to stay on theme, no matter what.

KAITLYN: It is theme-party season in New York, apparently. I guess it starts now and runs through Halloween? We have a roller-skating-and-disco-themed event next weekend, for Rebecca's 30th, and we are still waiting for the details on the Watergate-themed party that Andrew claims to be throwing in celebration of the event's 50th anniversary, which recently passed. Stephanie has been turning over summer yard-party themes in her mind for the entire pandemic, in pursuit of the perfect moment and the perfect theme for her triumphant return to hostessing. An Adam Sandler party has been imagined and discarded. An "album cover" party has been considered—wouldn't you like to see a girl painted up as Joni Mitchell's *Blue*? As *Hounds of Love*, including the dogs? At one time there was talk of "prom."

All to say that we knew that we would have a ton of fun on jubilee-and-murder day. If we didn't, well, then what were the next four months going to be like?

LIZZIE: All theme parties are different, obviously, but they're also kind of the same. Hosting one almost always comes with a long to-do list, and Claire set the standard even higher than usual. The morning of the party she sent

A

an email to the attendees confirming that "the Jubbly" would not be postponed on account of a few clouds and that there would be a royal banquet of food and drink available for consumption: mint and Earl Grey iced tea, "disgusting" gin and Dubonnet (apparently this is the Queen's favorite cocktail, and from my understanding it's essentially Mad Dog 20/20 mixed with gin), Pimm's, wine, beer, seltzer, canned cocktails, spiked chocolate-pudding shots, herb tea sandwiches, nova tea sandwiches, vegan cucumber sandwiches, an Eton mess trifle, a vegan trifle with coconut cream, mini pies, and five flavors of BjornQorn.

In this pre-party missive Claire also included links to some suggested reading materials on the Royal Family and related Jubilee rituals for any partygoers inclined to come prepared. Then, a reminder: "I'M NOT A MONARCHIST, I'M JUST A LOLER."

KAITLYN: I read that one on the train platform and I did LOL. The joke had a little something extra for me, I think, because I have lately been reading about actual American monarchists who are quite upsetting and are not interesting or hilarious thinkers at all. (Claire appreciates democracy and has nothing in common with those people . . . )

I was a bit antsy while going about my morning, I have to say. First of all, I had chipped a tooth earlier in the week, possibly on a frozen Oreo. And while I am generally amped to attend theme parties, a back-to-back party situation does present the challenge of "day drinking" and then "drinking at night also," which often ends in tears. To calm myself down I went to Crunch Fitness and did some lunges.

LIZZIE: I started the morning in New Jersey, having just attended a cousin's wedding. Walking through the World Trade Center from the PATH is its own kind of workout, where you need to avoid running into the people staring at the ceiling and ascend the weirdly slippery stairs without falling. I managed to make it to Claire's just 40 minutes past the 2 p.m. Jubbly call time.

The Jubbly was already in medium swing when we got there (Kait and I arrived together, by pure coincidence), and Claire's apartment was decked out in full Jubbly regalia: There was the promised table spread fit for high tea, banners of the Queen's face trimming Bernie the Landlord's vintage fireplace, and a six-foot branch wrapped in string lights playing the role of Prince Philip's favorite walking stick. This doubled as a visual gag and a potential photo prop for guests.

As the various groups of people in Claire's orbit started to mingle, I turned to some of my go-to conversation topics, like celebrity sightings and being pro overhead lighting. At one point I said, referring to some TV show,

A

"Something different happens every episode"—the sort of observational delicacy that really makes you wonder if I might qualify for some kind of award.

KAITLYN: Lizzie's overhead-lighting stance (again: pro) really shocked the room. My first order of business at Claire's was to apologize to Meredith and Julia for exposing them to strep throat when we had dinner at the Odeon more than 11 months ago. Next was to put on a plastic crown (not a monarchist!).

It rained just a little bit while we stood around eating our cucumber sandwiches and gin-infused chocolate pudding, talking about a real estate problem that I was dealing with, which was directly caused by a recent recipient of a MacArthur Genius Grant, not that anyone was really to blame. Lizzie and I counted the dogs present at the party—one, two, three, four! This never happens. If you're lucky there is one, *maybe* two dogs at a party. In attendance were: Claire's renowned dog Mars, whom I met once by accident while ruminating alone on a street in Bed-Stuy; Tiffany's dog Puddin', whom I knew from Instagram; and Darcie's dog Coco, whom I had seen on Twitter. The fourth dog I did not recognize, and we weren't introduced.

For the main party activity, Claire asked all her guests to pair up and complete wedding-vow-themed sheets of Mad Libs. Then each couple stood under a trellis and recited what they'd come up with, in hopes of winning a prize (Royal Family trading cards). They made promises like "to always play polo and record podcasts." Their vows were "briny" or "rotund." They got each other "wet and bothered." You get the picture! Liz and I typically are joiners but we sat in the corner and looked at our knees to avoid being called on because our Mad Lib was not good and we'd used the word booger. At one point Claire spun to look directly at us, shouting, "Hello over there!" We froze. But it turned out that there was a six- or seven-year-old boy standing behind us, separated from the party by a fence between his yard and Claire's, staring at everyone.

LIZZIE: My heart stopped then! It was a sign that maybe we weren't long for the Jubbly. We hastily said our goodbyes, as we still had places to go and people to see. On the walk home from Claire's, I stopped by Foodtown to get a Hal's New York Seltzer in Fruit Punch (delicious and confusing; my brain expected it to be thicker) and some sort of frozen mac-and-cheese-with-broccoli "meal" to quickly put on top of the cucumber sandwiches in my stomach before I had to rush out to the next party. I ate it while watching the first 15 minutes of *Fire Island*, then put on my most saloon-appropriate dress and shoved a too-small cowboy hat into my tote bag for the subway ride.

A

At this point my feet hurt from wandering the streets of New Jersey and Brooklyn all day (16,000 steps so far), but a true cowboy wouldn't let some barking dogs stop them from having a good time.

KAITLYN: I was also flagging during the theme-party interregnum, so I stopped by the McDonald's next to my apartment and grabbed a cheeseburger. Lately, I have been eating one cheeseburger a week. It makes me feel young!

En route to the Deadwood Saloon, I got into a dramatic text exchange with the outlaw Josey Wales, also known as Nathan. He had asked me earlier in the day to remind him of the address of the party, which I had refused to do, as he was copied on all of the same emails as I was. Well, that will teach me because he wound up at some random place in Bushwick with an address that bore absolutely no resemblance to the actual address of the party, which, again, was in Crown Heights (other side of the borough, for those who don't live here). "That's just what I had in my head," he said. Then he reasoned that it would not actually be disruptive to be substantially late because he was, after all, an outlaw, and therefore difficult to predict or pin down.

Sara—also known as Henrietta High-Stakes, the charming, shifty wife of the miserable saloon owner Harry High-Stakes—was very gracious about this suggestion and pretended that it made sense and that all was as desired.

LIZZIE: As for our characters: I was playing Banker Bonnie, a snooty rich lady and long-suffering wife of Banker Bob, an absentee husband and, in the case of this party, an absentee character. Kaitlyn was Poker Alice, a card dealer with a dark past working the saloon's poker tournament.

To begin the game, Sara handed out envelopes to each character that contained notes on our "objectives" for the evening, and fake money that we could use for extortion and bribery. This is also when the murderer was going to find out that they were, in fact, the murderer. From across the room, I heard Kaitlyn say, "I hope it's Liz." Well, if it was me, I knew who I would be killing first.

KAITLYN: Hey! Good luck, because as it turned out, Poker Alice was a secret former assassin.

I was actually shocked to learn that I was a violent criminal. The information was gradually revealed to me by others' aspersions throughout the party. What an odd experience! I was into it, though. I did feel some shame because, though Poker Alice's biography stated that she grew up in England, I had not managed to perfect my British American accent in time for the event. (I'd only gotten so far as saying "Lisa!" in the style of Connecticut native Dorit Kemsley.) Also, I blushed way too much when I was required to ask Billy the Bartender to confess his true love to me.

A

Still, I found my first murder mystery exhilarating because the conversations were all so lively and unpredictable. One second you're being blackmailed by a mysterious woman named Barb and the next she is explaining to you how she found her apartment, which is the ground floor of a converted cheese factory.

LIZZIE: I really liked Barb. In the game, Barb helped me stage a holdup at my bank, and in real life she's a jewelry designer.

I always say that I'm a better actor than Joaquin Phoenix, based on the performance I witnessed in the trailer for *Joker*, and this was the perfect opportunity to test that theory for a crowd. My Banker Bonnie had an accent that was probably inaccurate for the time period and, honestly, the patterns of human speech, but she was committed to living in the universe built by the anonymous storytellers at NightofMystery.com. I approached my objectives with the single-minded tenacity of a lamp-lover turning off the overhead light.

Around 9:30, we heard a scream and a character named Mitch fell dramatically to the floor.

KAITLYN: After Mitch was dead, someone outlined his corpse in masking tape and we took a break from the game. Mitch laid there on the floor while we sang "Happy Birthday" to Sara.

After this point, the game really took a turn for me. Everybody was given a new, blood-stained envelope with further tasks to perform, and it seemed, not to be self-centered, as if almost everyone's tasks involved accusing me of the murder or of a sexual affair. I didn't feel like I could be the murderer, and I honestly didn't know if I had participated in a sexual affair. So I just kept shouting that I was innocent and blew through all of my fake dollars bribing other people for their "secrets." Unfortunately, the secrets usually turned out to pertain to me and how I was the murderer or a participant in a sexual affair.

I suspected "Gambling Jack" or his wife or the sheriff or Barb of the crime, based on no evidence.

LIZZIE: My parents watch a lot of British murder mysteries, and I always like to try to guess who did it within the first 30 seconds of an episode. This time, because I was part of the action and not just a neutral observer, I felt incapable of fully grasping the plot or the cast of characters. Also, I was tired. Also, if this had actually been a British murder-mystery show, the murder would have been real and the victim wouldn't have been making jokes about crypto later that night.

I guessed wrong. I wasn't even close, honestly. Even after finding out who the culprit was, I didn't fully understand why. But I was happy to be Bonnie for the night and I'd do it again, if I could just get the accent right.

A

So we didn't solve the mystery at the Deadwood Saloon, but we did solve the mystery of how to attend multiple parties with pit stops in three neighborhoods and two states in just one day: Wear comfortable shoes, and for God's sake, don't drink too much Dubonnet.

KAITLYN: The murderer was a tall man named Mr. Money, whom I had never spoken to. Oh well!

# II

---

## GOSSIPING

# FREE WINONA

---

*May 2018*

KAITLYN: Lizzie was first to arrive at the party, which was in my yard. If your first question is "How can we expect Kaitlyn and Lizzie to write a fair and balanced review of a party hosted by Kaitlyn and invested in so eagerly by Lizzie?" well then, I'm sorry. There will be no satisfying answer for you.

According to the Facebook event, the party was Winona Ryder–themed.

LIZZIE: Who says this needs to be fair and balanced? It's not the complexion of a Sofia Coppola heroine! We (me, Frank, Matt) showed up to Kaitlyn's apartment a reasonable 15 minutes after the start time equipped with alcohol and a bag of Kit Kats. I think it's good form to show up to a friend's party slightly earlier than the majority of the guests are expected to arrive, in order to fill out the room. In this case, "the room" was the biggest residential backyard in Brooklyn.

KAITLYN: The main activities at the party were standing, drinking, eating Blow Pops, and listening to a Bose Mini.

Frank said, "Who is this?" And we said, "Rich Homie Quan." He said, "Can you spell it?" We spelled it. Five minutes later he said, "Who is this?" We said, "Nick Jonas." He said, "Can you spell it?" He was kidding! Frank told me he's in love. Frank wore a squid costume but he also wore a bachelorette party sash, making him part of Matt and Lizzie's costume, which was "bachelorette party." Matt was the bride and his name was Bride (pronounced bree-dah). They brought champagne, which I drank even though my costume also involved a Big Gulp cup full of Diet Coke and half a bottle of $8 rum. Bride said the orange decorations were ugly and they should have been pink. She said, "It's my day."

LIZZIE: Bride is what popular culture might refer to as a "Bridezilla," but she was very gracious about thanking everyone for attending her party. She only iced out the people who didn't bring her any gifts, which was pretty much everyone. She insisted she was getting married to an A-list celeb with the initials RG, but I don't know if I believe it.

Frank's squid costume consisted of three pairs of black tights stuffed with cotton balls tied around his waist, and a squid head that Matt sculpted out of paper, garbage bags, tiny Tupperware containers, and nail polish. Frank originally wanted to go as a "prolapsed anus" but the only prop we could come up with was a pink loofah. Ultimately we decided there just wasn't enough there.

KAITLYN: Everyone at the party was worked up because Winona Ryder was arrested once for shoplifting and it ruined her reputation. "What about a man's reputation, huh? Is there a way to ruin one of those?" Well, you won't get a satisfying answer to that question either. I can tell you that Chris Brown's new album is more than two and a half hours long.

LIZZIE: I don't remember engaging in much Winona Ryder– or Chris Brown–related chitchat, but I do remember this: The boy who showed up wasted, pulled a huge branch off a tree, and, in trying to throw the branch onto the bonfire, took down an entire string of party lights. I also remember that someone showed up dressed as that "Mr. Police, you could have saved her" subway ad for the Michael Fassbender movie *The Snowman*. It's all I want from a Halloween costume: really specific and dumb, with a shelf life of about half a day.

KAITLYN: Someone else was David S. Pumpkins, which I distinctly did not care for. None of my business. I was *Reality Bites* Winona which was just me in normal clothes plus a watch. Everyone at the party was worked up because someone's date was a Republican. He kept admitting it! I would say the Republican was famous, within the party. (He was also known as "the guy who pulled a huge branch off a tree, and, in trying to throw the branch onto the bonfire, took down an entire string of party lights.")

I had known he was coming and that he was a Republican, and I had learned how to build and sustain a campfire specifically so that he would not get the honor of participating in the task. But it didn't really deter him and no one gave me any credit.

LIZZIE: In the middle of every conversation Kaitlyn would get distracted by the fire she built, and walk toward it in a daze, as if she had accidentally invented it.

Next year I'm dressing up as anyone from that scene in *Garden State* where it's raining and they use trash bags as raincoats. It'll be really easy, plus incredibly dated, but not dated enough to seem nostalgic or cool. It'll just be like I got stuck in 2004 and am being held hostage by the Shins.

A

# LATKES, CAVIAR, PPCS

*December 2021*

KAITLYN: What did I bring to Ashley's casual holiday gathering in her and Bran's new apartment, which is actually a little bit closer to my apartment than her old apartment was but emotionally it feels farther because I have to get myself over Ocean Parkway? I'll tell you: *NOT* Melissa Clark's molasses-stout Bundt cake, which I prepared the night before while making insane final changes to my book, and which got stuck to the sides of the pan so badly that I had to claw it out with my claws. This was really humiliating because all the while that it was baking I was thinking, *Every woman should have a Bundt pan, it just makes anything look a little impressive, finally I have some really good advice to give to another homemaker.* Well, you know what they say about counting your chickens (don't), and about making plans under the watchful eyes of God (he'll laugh!). In the morning, I ended up hustling down to Avenue X to get some cheap caviar and some crème fraîche. I also picked up some classic Lays and some teeny-tiny bowls with teeny-tiny spoons at a nearby 99-cent store. (Melissa Clark says to use "small batch" potato chips for a chip-crème-caviar appetizer, but as I implied, we are on the outs.)

LIZZIE: I don't have a Bundt pan but if I do a mental scan of my kitchen cabinets, I can't think of anywhere one might fit. My landlord's architect (lol) gave me very narrow cabinets. Are Bundt pans unwieldy? They seem unwieldy. I do, however, like making things that look impressive. So I made Melissa Clark's "Perfect Black and White Cookies" and Carla Lalli Music's "Pink Party Cookies," or "PPCs." Matt helped glaze the B&Ws because he's more patient with sticky things and he has a steadier hand. They actually looked pretty good! I don't have a picture. Later I went over to Ideal Food Basket to get one of those aluminum trays to carry all the cookies in. Ideal, in its charmingly nonsensical way, stocks them next to the kitty litter, a little too high for me to reach comfortably. I feel like I'm always buying these aluminum trays, as if I run a catering business. Does anyone have a better way to transport a bunch of food to someone else's house when you have to take a bus there? It would've taken like seven plates to hold all these cookies. I also bought a bag of Doritos because I got worried our contributions to the party were too sugar-heavy.

KAITLYN: When Nathan and I arrived at the party we were unsurprisingly the very first ones there, having loitered on the corner of the street for several minutes waiting for it to be 3:59 p.m. Inside, the air was thick with onion because Bran was standing at the counter grating like 12 onions into a kiddie-pool-sized bowl. He claimed he felt fine because he was wearing contacts. I started weeping. Nathan left the room and came back a mess. Ashley apologized and I said something absolutely incoherent about how I love "behind-the-scenes vibes" and I always want to be seated near where the waiters keep their lighters and Diet Dr Peppers. I was crying so much!

LIZZIE: We got there around 5, I think. I was aiming for a fashionable but still inner-circle-y 4:30, but as I said earlier, we took the bus there, and the buses are only predictable in the sense that you can predict it will take longer for you to get there than you want it to, and longer than Google Maps says it will. While we were on the bus, an older woman came on ("came aboard"?) who happened to know the couple sitting in front of us. The meeting seemed spontaneous, but also planned. One half of the couple said to the woman as soon as she saw her, "Oh, this is for you," and handed her a bag before the woman was even able to sit down. I thought, *Since you're already comfortably sitting, why don't you just hold onto the bag for a sec until this woman can get settled, instead of burdening her with more items to hold on the bus?* I shouldn't really have an opinion. Honestly, the woman seemed fine with the extra bag. If I had to guess, I would say the bag was filled with cat stuff, because for the rest of the bus ride they talked about cats, and rescuing cats. That seemed to be how they were connected. They all got off at the same stop, which once again made me wonder why there was such a rush to hand off the bag. A few stops later we were at the party.

KAITLYN: I would say there were about six romantic couples in attendance, and a handful of hot, single people, and everyone was *so* nice except for Ashley and Colin when they were talking to each other about iPhone screen protectors. That was a tense moment and we didn't know where it was going. Perfect for a holiday party! I laughed all night and I stood up the whole time and I didn't take notes. I do remember a hot topic of conversation being the all-beef diet of a person who was not present—he grills the beef late at night at high heat, such that sizzling sounds can be heard throughout the apartment of someone who *was* present. Or he blends it up in a NutriBullet and drinks it like a smoothie.

LIZZIE: The smoothie-meat convo was a big moment. It felt like we were getting to the good stuff; the little gossips about nothing that really matters. Food-wise, there was also the biggest bowl of dip I've ever seen in my life, and some talk of Essentia water, if you consider that a food.

Someone said it had a "flat" flavor, and they meant it as a compliment.

KAITLYN: Ashley hugged and welcomed latecomers while simultaneously flipping latkes in boiling oil, which I thought was amazing and I told her so. Over the course of the night, Lizzie and I also luxuriated in compliments, not to brag. Multiple people were shocked that the party had some $7 caviar in the Doritos area and said, "Oh, caviar?" And then they ate a little bit of it, as a compliment to me, even though they didn't specifically know who had brought it or why. Similarly, a high-energy man came over to Lizzie and said, holding a PPC aloft, "What is this? It's the best thing I've ever eaten in my life." He was apparently serious. I laughed at that a lot, even though the PPCs were obviously phenomenal. Matt was like, "Someone take this guy to a restaurant."

LIZZIE: Of course I appreciated his enthusiasm, but there really was no magic baking secret here. The PPCs are basically just butter and sugar, two things that are known to taste good. If you creamed a bunch of sugar into butter and then ate it, you would probably be like, "Yeah, pretty good."

But I think the unbridled cookie enthusiasm is indicative of the party's general feeling. Everyone seemed at-ease, ready to mingle but not over-mingle, confidently content with wherever the night might take them. There was mood lighting, Kylie Minogue, and people who have known each other since high school, many of whom were doing something impressive in the medical or legal fields. We didn't get a lot of drama, but we did get a warm fuzzy feeling.

KAITLYN: This really was your classic intimate-holiday-celebration-and-housewarming. We learned a little bit about what kind of physics someone is studying in grad school. We tried to figure out exactly how tall each guest was by eye-balling it. We told everyone about our amazing idea for a podcast called *The Amazing Race* and they loved it. . . . At the start of each episode we pick a location in New York City, we bicker about the most efficient way to travel there, and then we see. The background noise of the City provides a rich soundtrack; our eventual reuniting at some great place like Goldie's Bar or Amelia's house in the Bronx serves as both reward and resolution. All the while, *The Verge*'s transportation reporter Andy Hawkins does little narrative bits about infrastructure and subway repairs and the dangers of riding a Citi Bike without a helmet. (Or at least he agreed to that role when we first started bringing this up all the time like five years ago.) You get it. You would love it. You would sort out the legal problems for us!

LIZZIE: The podcast idea comes up basically anytime we meet someone new. We really don't force it into the conversation; it's just that we always find ourselves in settings where people are talking about going somewhere. Sometimes I feel the need to say, "We know the name is taken," because often when we start our pitch you can see the question mark cloud their eyes.

It's relevant anyway to the end of the party, because I think the people who left the earliest had the longest train rides home.

KAITLYN: When a party starts at 4 p.m. in winter, you naturally think that it's 2 in the morning when it's actually only 7:45. Then, when you find out it's 7:45, you feel like you have your whole life in front of you!!!!! Of course, only a little while later it's 9:30 and all the wine bottles are empty and you're wondering what to do now that you've been drinking for five and a half hours on a stomach full of creamy dips. Well . . . whatever comes after that point is not a big secret but just a little bit of a secret and I don't want to talk about it right here.

# LIZZIE AND KAITLYN
# GO TO WILLIAMSBURG

---

*March 2022*

LIZZIE: For some reason Google Maps was telling us to take the C all the way to Broadway Junction, then get on the L and go back the other way to get to Grand Street. It seemed inefficient. Plus we had to carry a big cake and a nearly life-size cardboard cutout of the San Antonio Spurs mascot, known only as Coyote. I asked Matt why the mascot wouldn't just be a spur; it seems cleaner from a narrative perspective to keep all the symbols consistent, and I'm sure you could add some eyeballs to a spur if you needed it to be sentient. He didn't have a good answer. Anyway, all of these things—the L train, the cake, the cardboard Coyote—were coming into play because we had an invite to one of those events that seem to come around every few weeks in New York: the bar birthday party.

It was actually a surprise bar birthday party. A new take on an old standard. The planning happened in a group chat without me, but the gist of the thing was: Frank's birthday is coming up, but he may or may not be in Texas for his actual birthday. Maybe everyone could show up at a bar, and Susannah would lure Frank there for some made-up reason, and then we would yell "Surprise!" at him, or at least say it with gusto. The chosen bar was the unfortunately named Grimm Artisanal Ales, in Williamsburg. Both the name and the location really should make you think twice before going there on a Saturday night.

KAITLYN: I don't want to be rude, but I thought more than twice—probably a thousand times—before going to Grimm Artisanal Ales on Saturday night. I hate Williamsburg. The longest nights of my early 20s were spent forcing myself to find something to do there and then hanging on for dear life until 1 or 2 a.m. just so that I could plausibly claim to be "out," text the person I was dating that I was "out," then suggest that I was less than 20 minutes on foot from wherever he happened to be. It was so undignified . . . and Kellogg's Diner may be where they filmed one of the best episodes of HBO's *Girls*, but it isn't a good diner at all.

I was thinking about this as I made my way—at a glacial place—to the party, opting to walk from the first L stop in Brooklyn and to pause for a drink at a cozy-looking bar that smelled like wood chips. I immediately sloshed a bit of vodka gimlet onto my library book, which was the new 832-page one about Watergate. I believe I am the first person to borrow it, so the slosh will be easy to trace! A bunch of 22-year-old girls at the other end of the otherwise empty bar were arguing about who had paid for the last round of shots and who would pay for the next one. They were friends with the bartenders, like on a TV show. I'm sure some of them were texting love interests. I was texting Lizzie saying I was on my way but I was also thinking some dark thoughts, along the lines of, *Do I wish I was still that young?* And then, unfortunately, *Maybe I do, and I'm going to be sick.*

I was feeling sorry for myself, like Nixon. But, also like Nixon, I was gonna fight. . . . So I pulled myself together and walked the last few blocks to Grimm. Lizzie was there already, wearing a white button-down with tiny white suspenders and eating a "chopped cheese" taco.

LIZZIE: What can we say about Grimm Artisanal Ales? As much as I don't love the name, I can't say it's misleading. If you're the kind of person who might want to drink something that could be classified as an "artisanal ale," you'll find yourself with lots of options here. It's also big, which is a good thing sometimes, like if you need to hide. There was a cat wandering around, who seemed to belong to the brewery, and lots of dogs who didn't seem to care that there was a cat.

Kait and I ordered our pét-nats (even though we felt like ordering beer would've been more supportive of the

A

establishment) and split a lime weed gummy. Just as we were starting to feel settled, a man walked up to us and leaned over the table, angling his phone toward Coyote like it was Adrian Grenier at the airport. "I need to take a picture of your bunny here," he said.

KAITLYN: To be clear, if we haven't been, the coyote (not bunny!!) was a birthday surprise for Frank, who is from San Antonio. Matt designed it on his computer and had it made by some guy with a huge printer in Manhattan. The coyote's jersey featured the logo of a Texas grocery-store chain, but Matt had edited it to read *Celebrating Frank, 1984–2022*. To an onlooker, this might make it seem as though Frank had died. Well, he hadn't. While we were waiting for him, Matt explained that Frank has "the most goals in soccer," which turned out to mean that he has the current goal-scoring record in one of the Brooklyn soccer leagues for super-athletic adults. So pretty much the opposite of dead, I would say.

The waiting period of a surprise party is so interesting. We were not more than one or two drinks into it when Lizzie broached the topic of how long she would mourn Matt if he were to be killed in a freak accident. Matt said, "For one day you wouldn't do the Wordle," but Lizzie denied that. She didn't say how many Wordles she felt she would actually skip.

LIZZIE: Aren't we going to run out of Wordles in like a year anyway? This is why when *The New York Times* spent a bunch of money on it, I thought, *Isn't that like spending a bunch of money on the water inside a humidifier?* It's going to all be gone eventually.

At some point, someone got the "We're 2 minutes away" text from Susannah, meaning the birthday boy's arrival was imminent. Everyone turned to watch the door.

Frank and Susannah walked in and had to do the ol' ID and vax card scramble. It was clear Frank hadn't seen us yet. How exciting for me! I've never seen the face of a truly surprised person before, and I had time to prepare for it. I was staring very hard at Frank's face to make sure I didn't blink when the surprise registered.

I'll tell you this: Surprise looks a lot like confusion turning into joy, but that's based on a single data point.

KAITLYN: My concern when Frank and Susannah were arriving was that Frank wouldn't immediately remember who I was, having only met me a few times over the course of five years. I didn't want him to look at the group and think, *Is this a surprise birthday party for me? I don't want to make an embarrassing assumption . . . and I don't know who that person is . . . so maybe the party is for someone else.*

But he did remember who I was! And he grasped what was happening!

Phew. My second or third drink was a beer but it had Pinot Noir grapes in it, so it was basically still wine. I loved it. I also loved listening to Lizzie explain the terribly complicated premise and gameplay process of *Deal or No Deal* to someone who had never seen it, and I loved when Susannah expressed sincere surprise that nobody else at the table had bothered to customize their Reddit aliens to look like themselves. I took a picture of her brandishing her user profile on her phone and put it on my Instagram story, captioned "All girls are on Reddit!" It's one of those things that seems like it could be true.

LIZZIE: *Deal or No Deal* and Reddit are alike in a lot of ways, or at least alike in one very significant way: Once you get sucked in, it's really hard to get out.

Here's what else we covered, conversationally:

- Craigslist roommates, and how sometimes they turn out to be really good friends, but most of the time you stop talking to them after your lease ends because you had to dodge them while they did pull-ups in the doorway of the kitchen too many times. Karen told a story about her roommate getting the exact same "really ugly" tattoo as her in the exact same spot years after they stopped living together. This was the same roommate who had previously written about the size of Karen's breasts in her LiveJournal entries.

- The former *Summer House* castmate Hannah Berner and her Irish-comic fiancé, Des Bishop. Someone had spotted them at Gowanus's Pig Beach a few months prior. Pig Beach is generally the place you go when you can't find outdoor seating at any other bar but you absolutely must sit at a picnic table and spend $21 on a frozen cocktail. I wonder if the combination of the cornhole and the Virginia Beach meets casual Friday attire that's so common there took her back to her days in front of the Bravo cameras.
- The sound a cow makes while being killed by a coyote. This one was from Kaitlyn.

KAITLYN: Okay, I don't mean to bring this up all the time, but I've become really concerned about the coyotes that live behind my parents' house. I don't think it is a good sign that they wander around in daylight now!

The next thing that happened may surprise you. . . . I was moved by the weed gummy to approach a man at the bar who was reading one of those Library of America books that have a ribbon for keeping track of your page. I felt a powerful curiosity about him because he was having an artisanal beer in a well-lit room while people around him were shout-laughing and breaking glasses, and he didn't seem to be experiencing any stomach-twisting or dark thoughts. He was reading Wendell Berry, he said. I said, "Oh!" and that I'd started to read the recent *New Yorker* profile, but had gotten annoyed—not everyone can just own a bunch of land, even if they save money by not having toilets. People are right to live in cities, I said. He was not defensive at all and told me he knew where I was coming from but there were several reasons I might give Berry a try anyway, if I had the time.

I really had to sit down after that. I was like, *That was shocking?* If an obviously drunk person had come up to me at a bar and asked what I was reading, I would have assumed they were making fun of me. I would have told them to get the hell out of my face. No one else was really dwelling on it, but I felt changed. I ate my cake and listened to a confusing but exhilarating story about how Susannah was blocked on Instagram by the poet Rachel Rabbit White for some reason, but she can still see her Stories by logging in to her dog's account. This is how she learned that Rachel Rabbit White moved into Caroline Calloway's apartment, surely a mistake considering Calloway had supposedly painted over all the cabinets and the microwave. (She said.)

Anyway, I waltzed out early on a high note to meet Nathan and his friends Rebecca and Bayne in Bushwick. They said they'd just been to KGB Bar and that someone had taken the Soviet flag off of the wall and ceremoniously torn it in half, in solidarity with Ukraine. I said I didn't know if people need to be doing all that. Then I spaced out for, like, 90 minutes.

LIZZIE: The rest of us stayed at the bar until last call, which at Grimm Artisanal Ales is only midnight. That was our signal to head out. If we learned anything, it was that you can't fake a surprise, you can't fake the sound of a coyote getting killed by a cow, and you can't fake a good time. Luckily, we didn't have to!

KAITLYN: In the words of Richard M. Nixon: "Dignity, command, faith, head high, no fear, build a new spirit, drive, act like a President, act like a winner." In bed by 12:45!

# PARTY FOR *THE DRIFT*,
# A COOL NEW MAGAZINE

*March 2022*

KAITLYN: Being a hater takes years off of your life, so it's better to try to be a fan. When I first heard about *The Drift,* the new magazine for young intellectuals, I had a knee-jerk negative reaction due to internship trauma—in 2014, I worked hundreds of unpaid hours for another magazine that was going to breathe life back into American political and literary discourse, but turned out to be a ridiculous operation run by jerks. I'm also defensive about the suggestion that all of the uncool magazines that have been around since, oh, say, 1857, are staffed by skittish prudes who wouldn't dare to touch the outré ideas that a cool new magazine must dedicate itself to championing. (Both of these are clearly "me problems.")

But I like magazines in general because I like reading. I also like parties: I like to be part of what's going on, especially if I can do so in a way that won't involve actually doing or saying anything myself. If I can stand in a room and sip a drink and be counted . . . that's perfect. So I paid $15 plus fees for a ticket to *The Drift*'s Issue Six launch party at the Jane Hotel in Manhattan, and I asked Lizzie if she would go with me.

LIZZIE: I, of course, said yes. "I'll do anything" is what I always say. And it's sort of true. If I'm being all the way honest, which I guess I should be here, I didn't really know what *The Drift* was when I accepted the invite. But I knew that we were going to the "Issue Six Launch Party" and I'm not a dumbass, so I figured it was going to be a launch party for something with issues, i.e., a magazine.

It wasn't until we were standing in line outside the Jane, when Kaitlyn mentioned that the heavy crowd might be the result of a recent *New York Times* profile, that I had a flicker of recognition. I hadn't read the profile, but I remembered clocking the photo of the founders, which looks like it was taken on a really cold day. It made me wonder what it would be like to pose next to a tree with a scarf on in 20-degree weather while a *New York Times* photographer told me not to smile. Not everyone knows this about me, but I don't really like nature the way some people do, or the way nature tends to look when it's cold out. I hope I never have to pose next to a winter tree. This was the extent of my familiarity with *The Drift*, which is to say, I was not familiar. Once we made it inside the hotel, new bits of information dribbled out and I tried to hold on to what I could. The ticket collector at the door handed me a free copy of Issue Six (included in the ticket price), but he couldn't figure out if Kaitlyn should also get a copy, because she bought her ticket in advance. Eventually he did give her a copy, but he did it begrudgingly.

KAITLYN: That guy could be the next West Elm Caleb: He was in the wrong, he made me feel bad, and I bet other people had the same experience with him! But I won't talk about it anymore. I don't even know how to make a Tik-Tok. . . . Anyway, getting into this party was really an ordeal. The doors supposedly opened at 7 p.m., which may have been true, but nobody was allowed to walk through them until 7:30. (Lizzie was like, "*The Drift?* More like the seconds of our lives are drifting by . . .") You also couldn't enter without getting stamped by a large "Jane Hotel" stamp that included the building's address—zip code and everything—in case, I guess, someone found you later in the Hudson River and needed to know where to return you. This was exciting, to be honest. A little macabre, like the interior of the Jane Hotel.

Once inside I was thrilled to take a photo of a taxidermied white peacock, which reminded me of Martha Stewart's recently liberated peafowl. Then we wriggled our way up to the bar, near a taxidermied monkey in a little hat, and waited many minutes to order an Old Fashioned for me and a Peroni for Liz. (I don't normally drink Old Fashioneds, but I wanted something I could sip slowly, which would give me something to do with my hands for the whole party.) "It'd be cool if there was no one here," Lizzie said. She wasn't being mean. She only meant it literally: It was a dim, romantic room to settle into for a drink with no one else around. A person could really indulge her inner life, do some fantasizing, write down some secrets. Not tonight, though!

Meanwhile, Julia was stuck outside in the line. "This is hellll on earth," she texted, reporting that people were becoming disgruntled. There was nothing we could do for her.

LIZZIE: We agreed that it was totally understandable that Team *Drift* would want to have a launch party at the Jane. It's got that haunted, old-money vibe, the lighting is flattering, and, as we already mentioned, there's lots of interesting taxidermy to look at. Sometimes you even get to see tourists rolling their Away luggage through the lobby. Totally understandable. And yet, it started to become obvious pretty quickly that the crowd was going to keep getting bigger all night long, while the room, well, the room wasn't getting any bigger at all. I've never been able to estimate crowd numbers or distance in meters, but it felt like there was enough seating for only 12 people and enough people to fill some mid-tier, emotionally draining music venue like Terminal 5. We found some empty space under the stairs, which gave us a pretty good view of the scene.

KAITLYN: There were all sorts of well-dressed women, lots of different types of boys in glasses, and, of course, hundreds of tote bags on a spectrum from Telfar to *The Baffler*. From our spot under the stairs, I could see Lake, the sole other person I knew at the party, but I would have had to leap over at least two velvet couches and three coffee tables to say hello to him, so I never did. I hope he had a nice evening!

The readings were short and sweet. The first one was an excerpt from an essay about the state of the essay, which I'd already read online with my mouth open, thinking *This really hits me where it hurts.* (See: "The essayists leave behind a mess of maybes and perhaps and hot, urgent rhetorical questions that dare you to scream yes! or no! or sure, why not, who cares!") The second was an excerpt from an essay about the CGI influencer Lil Miquela. It was funny and good, though Lil Miquela has been the subject of essays for more than four years already. Not to be a hater.

LIZZIE: I did appreciate the swiftness of the reading portion of the evening, which lasted about 30 minutes, but the brevity was achieved only by giving each writer just a few minutes to read their work, which meant we (the audience) were getting excerpts. Aesthetically, I have no problem with excerpts. I love a good tease and I've never read all of *Moby-Dick*. But because I hadn't read any of the Issue Six essays or fiction prior to hearing them read out loud to me in pieces, the experience was something like being blindfolded, thrown in the trunk of a car, and dropped off at an unrecognizable location: The place may look nice enough, but you can't pretend you're not lost. I'd like to stress that this really had nothing to do with the writing and more to do with the fact that my brain switches to the white-noise channel at almost every reading I go to unless I'm looking for a good cry, and I was distracted by a painting on the wall that looked like blood was seeping through it from the other side.

When the readings were over, the crowd really did seem very excited to dive into the rest of Issue Six on their own time.

KAITLYN: "I'm here," Julia texted. But she couldn't be found.

We had a series of miscommunications with her—which ficus we were near, which end of the bar she was standing at—that went on for about 20 minutes. All along, the crowd was growing. People were trying to be polite, but there was no way to walk around that didn't involve some shoving. We decided we would not move and Julia would have to look for us. While we waited, Lizzie tried to take a picture and the flash went off, forcing her to throw her body on top of the camera that was in her own hand. This woke us up a bit and we started looking

A

around for ways to participate. We thought, *Should we do some reporting?* "Oh, Christian Lorentzen is behind you," I told Lizzie. She said she didn't know what he looked like. I said that he looked like the person standing behind her. Then I said, "I wondered if he would be here, since he tweeted earlier today, 'Yeah, yeah, I'll be there.'" As soon as I said that, I was pretty embarrassed about it, and that was the end of the night's journalism.

LIZZIE: I didn't recognize anyone, but like I said, I don't know who anyone is and I need a new glasses prescription. For the next bit of time, it felt like a lot of my mental capacity was taken up by the act of inching around every few seconds to accommodate new groups of people trying to squeeze past, through, or around me.

KAITLYN: At last, Julia popped out of the crowd. She'd just bought a gin and tonic for a stranger, she told us, and was regretting it because it cost $16. Lizzie said she should take comfort in coming off like a big shot. I told her that the money would find its way back to her—something to do with quantum physics. At this point I was eating the maraschino cherries and orange wedge out of the bottom of my drink and dreaming in a big way about dinner.

Before we left, we surveyed the room, feeling rude, trying to work out the percentage of the guests who were really going to go home and read their new copies of *The*

*Drift* from cover to cover. This, like all things, made me feel sad about getting older. I still have the copy of *n+1* I got at the first magazine party Lizzie and I ever attended together in a boutique hotel, and I did read every single page of it because I was young, curious, impressed; had a lot of free time; and was not yet grumpy or jealous. Was I once . . . an angel?

LIZZIE: As much as Kait thinks things change, I'm sure they pretty much stay the same, because I would bet money I never read most of that issue of *n+1*. It's not that I don't appreciate a quality paper stock or a saucy essay, but I'm always chasing the high of the 2007 music issue of *The Believer* that came with a CD and might have included that essay about the reclusive musician turned telemarketer Bill Fox. I think about it all the time. Like Kaitlyn a few years ago, I was young, curious, and impressed back then.

We left the hotel and walked past a line of people outside still waiting to get in. That was the most confusing part of the night! I couldn't tell you what they were hoping to find once they got inside, except the opportunity to do coke in a 90-degree bathroom. As we walked down Jane Street, each of us (me, Julia, Julia's friend Rebecca) took turns trying to convince Kaitlyn that whatever sentiment she regretted saying out loud would be forgotten the next day, or even sooner.

KAITLYN: "It's not my job to be cool," I told everyone while we wandered around the West Village, led by Julia's false sense of where the martini bar Dante's was located. This has become something of a mantra for me. When we finally found the bar, I ordered a bright pink cosmopolitan with a chunk of strawberry in it. *Not my job to be cool*, I thought to myself. *Not my job to be cool.*

# III

---

## GALLIVANTING

# WEEKEND AT RUBY'S

*November 2019*

KAITLYN: Another miracle of Gchat group travel planning, this year's fall trip was to a town that had (1) farm festival, (1) winery, (1) haunted church tour, and 100,000 canvas prints from Pier 1 Imports, all hanging up in our personal "ranch house" at the corner of Sheep Pasture Road and Old Town Road (yes!). My favorite was a "painting" of a baby tiger looking down at his reflection in a puddle of water and seeing a full grown tiger. My second favorite was four Eiffel towers.

LIZZIE: We realized in one of our 32 Lyft rides subsidized by Ashley's access to a seemingly infinite promotion that this was our 4th Annual Fall Trip. The only other things I've done for four years straight is high school, college, and pap smears.

We can't miss a fall trip now, it's too important. In just four years, we've created a dangerous, nearly untenable situation in which we must either continue the tradition forever or else risk the dissolution of the friendship. Unfortunately, in what may have been a warning, Kaitlyn offhandedly mentioned the possibility of us all having a major fall out in the future.

Well, we were originally planning on going to the Hamptons or the Berkshires, but everything was out of our price range as three working women with a lot of weddings to go to this year. We ended up getting a last-minute deal of a lifetime on an Airbnb in Stony Brook, Long Island. The listing promised a cozy home with a rabbit in the basement and no cable or Wi-Fi or entertainment of any kind.

KAITLYN: As soon as we arrived, we waited 15 to 20 minutes for the teenager who was cleaning the bathrooms to leave, then we unlocked the basement door, snuck down there in a single file line, past a giant whiteboard with a month's worth of an absolutely insane workout routine outlined on it (on the first day you do a 30-second plank and on the 30th day you do a 10-minute plank? Get real!) and over to a large pen, with a fence about the height of a baby gate, which did not seem nearly tall enough.

I was in front, and I don't know how it happened. I'm not a leader by nature, as you know, and I'm also not even particularly curious about the world around me, so who can say. I rounded the corner of the pen and peered into a half-eaten cardboard box, which is where I looked directly into the red eyes of a 30-pound white rabbit. "No," I said to Ashley and Lizzie as I walked quickly but calmly back toward the psychotic gym area (5 push-ups on day one and 100 push-ups on day 30??). "I don't like her," I said, I think firmly enough for them to comprehend.

Nobody listened to me. On the whiteboard, I pointed out to no one, there was also a reminder to attend a screening of *Avengers: Endgame*, which made it seem like nobody had been downstairs in months, maybe for a specific reason. . . . I may as well have been writing the words in the air with my finger, and facing into the corner like a *Blair Witch* kid. Ashley and Lizzie walked over to the box and looked inside and cooed like they were looking at their own newborn children. They loved the rabbit. Her name was Ruby and they talked about her constantly for the rest of the trip.

LIZZIE: Airbnb should actually pay us for wanting to stay in a rabbit's bachelor pad in the middle of nowhere so badly. The house was everything we ever wanted and more. The fridge was full of carrots. Ashley was a little scared because I had to kill a giant cricket in the living room basically as soon as we got there and it brought up some cricket trauma from her past. She also didn't like the fuzzy blanket on the bed we all planned to sleep in. Kaitlyn said something genius, which was, possibly paraphrased: "I think you're mistaking aesthetic displeasure for fear." It really resonated with me, because this is exactly what happens to me with Mr. Bean!

After a brief tour of our aesthetically challenged home, we headed out to a harvest festival at a local farm. As far as I can tell, farm living is exactly like they say it is in the movies.

KAITLYN: Yes, with Ruby on our minds, we went to a farm called Benner's Farm, and looked at goats, pigs, chickens, you name it. Ashley was particularly infatuated with the first pig we saw, but then we saw a much larger pig and she didn't even care about the other one anymore. We paid $1 each for a haunted hayride with very little hay (it was more like a wooden bench ride) and very many hauntings—the tractor driver, who was perhaps 60, started the ride saying, "My dad put up a bunch of figures in the woods. At the end, tell me which is your favorite." At the end, most of the parents with young children were like. . . . "We liked the pumpkins?" The "figures" were all more terrifying than I can possibly describe, but I'll give you a taste: In one scenario there was a 20-foot tall spider web strung across several trees, full of body-sized "bodies" wrapped up in spider stuff, with only their pumpkin or demon mask faces showing. Many of the figures had yellow, spindly fingers with mutated, swollen fingertips, but we couldn't figure out what they were made of.

Um, anyway, we posed in a plywood cut out so our faces were replacing three peas in "peas in a pod!" Then we bought $2 dixie cup coffees from a teen girl in a

A

cozy-looking hoodie, who yelled at a teen boy in a cozy-looking hoodie because he spilled water on a power strip and almost killed them all. I became emotional, obviously, listening to them bicker—I loved being that young! It was still hilarious to call a boy you liked a "butthole." You could think about your crush all day long. You had no responsibilities other than helping him stay alive!

To remind us (me) that we're adults now—with debit cards, and nice sweaters, and at least a couple romantic prospects among us that know better than to drench their electronics—we set off to get drunk at a vineyard on the side of some body of water.

LIZZIE: The wines of Long Island are among the worst I've ever put in my mouth, but at least we were also in Long Island. Some men in flip flops bought a bottle of the red that tasted like melted plastic (I think it was a 2016 vintage) and made disgusted faces as soon as they drank it. They were right to be disgusted, but they were wrong to have purchased an entire bottle from the winery, which did offer tastings for a sum of money some might consider overly confident.

KAITLYN: It's true. I don't believe in Yelp reviews or diminishing the work of small business owners but tasting four wines at Harmony Vineyards in St. James, New York, costs $21? And each wine is scarier than the last. We started out with what tasted like a gas station Chardonnay—okay fine! We're not even snobs! But as we descended into various reds, we started noticing something odd: "notes of banana," "notes of caramel swirled with cherry and garlic," "notes of lilac laundry detergent." I'm joking about the last one and the second-to-last one, but literally it said "notes of banana" on the laminated card. Banana! This was the most disgusting wine anyone has ever tasted or will ever taste. When I think of how it may have been made I see a man throwing stray pieces of licorice and a bottle of acetone into one of those huge Gatorade water coolers and then pausing, "Oh, grapes!"

There were a lot of dogs at Benner's Farm, but we didn't have time to look at them because Ashley only wanted to hear facts about the 615-pound hog and I only wanted to watch the teenagers interact with each other. There were also dogs at Harmony Vineyards, which would normally have made Lizzie pretty happy, but she was distracted by how much she hated a man with an acoustic guitar who was positively screaming "Mr. Brightside" at us in the middle of the afternoon, and by wrapping her little fist around the tasting glasses, crushing them to powder one at a time.

LIZZIE: Who needs a dog when you have Ruby?

KAITLYN: See what I mean? She's obsessed with Ruby!

LIZZIE: Because part of the fun of fall trip is packing as many activities as we can into a single Saturday in October, we went right from the horrors of Long Island wine to the horrors of the local historical society's graveyard tour. We paid more than you might expect to see members of the historical society dressed in their finest period attire, doing impressions of historically significant (and dead) locals.

Some volunteer actors stumbled over their lines so clumsily, I was forced to stare into the ground until I started seeing through the grass to the actual dead people. Our tour guide didn't know the route she was supposed to take us on, and we kept getting lost. It was during one of these unplanned detours that Kaitlyn said something like, "I keep wondering what kind of huge fight we'll get into that'll finally put an end to this whole friendship thing."

KAITLYN: I was just protecting myself. This tour was incredibly long, it was all about seemingly randomly chosen people who grew up in Long Island, it was not scary at all, and I felt like Lizzie and Ashley may have resented me for finding the East Setauket Facebook events page and suggesting that we waddle through a freezing tour of two different Protestant churches at which apparently several Confederate sympathizers are buried and nobody thinks it's a problem to dress up as them and tell their charming life stories at a modern-day fundraiser. Things got even worse once a woman on the tour took it upon herself to shine an LED flashlight directly into Lizzie's face for several minutes at a time, whenever she least expected it. On the bright side (haha), a couple of the stories were, if not exactly scary, at least deeply fucked up. One of the ghosts told us about how she rescued her alcoholic boyfriend from a boat incident on Christmas Eve and, rather than risking social judgment by taking him back to her normal house, went with him to his drunken bum shack, which is where they "spent the night" wrapped in her shawl and then woke up dead. They froze to death!

So, at this point, Ashley selected a restaurant for us called Pasta Pasta.

LIZZIE: Pasta Pasta surprised us all with its stunning decor and its massive portion size. You should definitely go if you ever get the chance. I think it's a chain. In the end, Pasta Pasta and the Stony Brook Winery really did us a solid by feeding us so many carbs and so much poison wine that we were all able to sleep soundly that night in our haunted rabbit cottage.

KAITLYN: I don't remember anything about Pasta Pasta other than the fact that there were beta fish all over the place, in every vase. There were also pink Christmas lights on every surface because it was breast cancer awareness month. We ate at least four pounds of calamari, plus garlic bread, plus pastas of all shapes and sizes, along with a bottle of wine I forced Lizzie to select since everything that had gone wrong during the rest of the day-long trip had been pretty obviously my fault. We slept three peas in a pod in a California King, and we'll never know exactly where Ruby slept. She could have been anywhere : )

LIZZIE: Before we fell asleep in our single bird's nest of a bed, Kaitlyn said we should share secrets. She went first, and then we fell asleep.

KAITLYN: The next day I went on a date in an oyster bar and started to complain about this behavior on Ash and Liz's parts, but then my date said, "What was the secret?" And I was like, oh, this is how they're going to get away with it. I'm never going to bring it up again because I never want to remind them of what I said. I hope they forget to read this newsletter!

Anyway, the odds of a fifth fall trip have never been higher. Unless we have a big falling out.

# IS VAL DAY THE BEST
# DAY IN NEW YORK?

*February 2022*

KAITLYN: Years ago, our friend Tamar was seeing a boy who had three or four odd qualities. I'm only going to state one of them here because otherwise he will be instantly identifiable and may become angry: He wouldn't say "Valentine's Day"; instead he said "Val Day," which we absolutely loved.

Now, look, I grew up in the suburbs, and like everyone else I have trauma from never receiving a carnation from my crush during homeroom and never being offered a promise ring or whatever by my one true love. Valentine's Day as a teenager is brutality. Val Day in New York City, however, is a different story. They sell roses in tents by the subway. They sell teddy bears out of the backs of vans. The restaurants have cupids and arrows painted on the windows . . . grown-ups eat candy and heart-shaped baguettes! Oh, and my eyes just fill with tears because Val Day in New York City is for everyone; it is so beautiful, and we call it Val Day because a boy with odd qualities offered us the term and then, after some weeks, sweetly disappeared from our lives.

A

So imagine all that, and then, I'm sorry to ask, imagine it is 20 degrees and windy and you're headed down to the water in the dark.

LIZZIE: A cold, questionable journey toward an icy body of water that could swallow you alive without anyone noticing feels a lot closer to how I've always experienced Val Day in New York City than my bright-eyed friend Kaitlyn here. I don't mean to sound cynical—I understand the appeal of gooey, medicinal-tasting chocolates in a heart-shaped box, and I appreciate the unearned glow of early infatuation, but I also find it hard to love anything at all about the month of February, and roses just remind me of funerals. My mind is a battlefield.

This frigid walk to the water we're alluding to is the one from Eighth Avenue to the Hudson River, which you have to do if you wanted to, for example, go on a Valentine's Day cruise in New York Harbor. And we did. We were going to drink champagne on a boat called the *Manhattan II*, and nothing—not frozen ears, seasickness, public makeout sessions, or technical difficulties—was going to stop us.

KAITLYN: The cost of two tickets on Classic Harbor Line's Valentine's Day Champagne Tasting Cruise, including tax and a reasonable tip, is $346. If you've ever been outside your house you know that this is more money than basically any 90-minute activity other than surgery should cost, and also enough money to buy a very nice dinner inside a building.

But there is a time in some of our lives—if we appear to be young men who work in finance, for example—when we want to spend a ludicrous amount of money on our special someones and provide them with an experience that we did not have to put any effort into planning, yet can conceivably be labeled "romantic" and "thoughtful." During those dear, brief days, $346 is just the right price, and Pier 62 in 20-degree weather is just the right place. Maybe! (Or, as was the case for me and Lizzie, maybe we just want to do something new and odd in the city we love.)

Pier 62 is on the river at 22nd Street, across from an enormous gymnastics gym. While we stood around, Lizzie and I watched through the window as 10-year-olds did front flips. We shivered and stomped our feet, saying how terrible it was to be a child and have no control over how you spend your time. Though the children looked warm. And one of them was doing oblique crunches while she waited for her turn to use some apparatus, so I guess she liked being there and was dedicated to her craft. We were still glad to be spending our time precisely as we'd chosen to: freezing to death among other adults, including a young woman who was wearing a dress and no tights, a young woman who was flopping backward

A

into her boyfriend and pulling his hands into her coat pockets, a young woman who was holding a dozen yellow roses and looking grim, and a bunch of young men in nice jackets.

LIZZIE: As is often the case with activities involving departure times, our ticket instructions dictated that we should plan to arrive at the dock anywhere from 15 to 30 minutes early, for no real reason other than to raise the stakes of our journey with a little frostbite play. We were supposed to board five minutes prior to our scheduled departure, but this didn't happen.

Everyone was antsy. When a nearby boat blew its little horn, some enterprising ticket-holders decided that it must have been a call for us to board, and they lined up accordingly. Kaitlyn and I muttered that this seemed a little overconfident. These were not boat people—as a viewer of Bravo's various *Below Deck* franchises, I can promise you that—and the boat with the horn wasn't even that close to us.

The man in the ticket booth (a boat person) had to announce that we were, in fact, being too eager. Our boat was having some technical difficulties, but they hoped to have us boarding "in a matter of time." Perceptive readers might recognize that this is not actually a meaningful measurement of time—everything that has ever happened has happened in a matter of time.

In reality, it was about 10 more minutes before we boarded.

The *Manhattan II* seems to take its design inspiration from Bass Pro Shops: a lot of light wood, dark-green upholstery, and vintage-looking floatation devices. We sat at our designated table, shielded from our serious-looking young tablemates by a sheet of plexiglass.

KAITLYN: Todd, who described himself as our second mate, gave a speech about the ways in which this boat was "a little different than a land restaurant." The key differences were that we needed to remember where the life jackets were and that we were to treat our champagne glasses as our "pet rocks," meaning we had to take them with us if we went out onto the deck or into the bathroom, so that they couldn't slide around and shatter in our absence. Also, we were to wear masks. Needless to say, several couples heard this last directive and then totally ignored it—some so that they could make out, which is one thing, but others just so they could sit there without masks on, for whatever reason they were telling themselves, which is another.

LIZZIE: By this time, I started to notice a small surge of nausea starting to creep up, and it wasn't from seeing the lower half of our shipmates' faces. We were experiencing a classic case of boat turbulence, but not one I was prepared for. Luckily, Kait found some pretzels and an unmarked blister pack of chewable tablets loose at the bottom of her tote bag that she thought might be Dramamine. I love Dramamine. Can't get enough of the stuff. I Googled the active ingredient listed on the foil packaging: "Alcohol: Avoid. Very serious interactions can occur." I popped one and let the chalky generic berryness settle in my molars, ready to taste some champagne . . .

KAITLYN: The first glass was a pretty good sparkling Chardonnay from the Hudson Valley. I enjoyed it but I was disoriented by my utter ignorance of where we were in physical space. First, I incorrectly identified what must have been New Jersey as Brooklyn, thinking that we were in the East River, even though that wouldn't make any sense. I then incorrectly identified the Empire State Building as the Freedom Tower. At one point, Lizzie saved us by recognizing the Colgate Clock, but we were soon lost again. It didn't help that the boat made several sharp turns.

Before our second glass of champagne, a server dropped off a little cup of water crackers and told us we were at a very lucky table. "The people who sat there on the last cruise got engaged," he said.

LIZZIE: He clearly intended this nugget of information to make us feel special, to encourage us to believe in the romantic power of the yacht, and perhaps even to feel as if we had been struck by the fishing spear of Nautical Cupid ourselves. Mostly it just made us feel like we missed our only chance to experience a major Valentine's Day moment, all due to a circumstance of scheduling. What if we had booked the earlier boat ride? What if they had booked the later one? Like ships in the night, I tell you!

The water crackers our server gave us were followed by a plate of three cheeses, each meant to pair with our next three glasses of champagne. The cheese plate, like me and Kaitlyn after we found out we missed a front-row seat to a marriage proposal, was a little deflated. The cheeses sat on a thin bed of no more than five pieces of wilted arugula, surrounded by a bird's handful of dried goji berries, three olives, and two pieces of dried peach. The cheeses had the kind of pungent aroma capable of completely derailing a romantic evening, but we were starving, and so we dutifully ate what we could. There was something "airplane meal" about it all. Like eating a cheese plate in a spacious Boeing with an area rug, going around in circles.

KAITLYN: I don't think we wanted or expected a lot more, but we had expected some chocolate. Chocolate was specifically mentioned on the website.

Of course, what we were really there for was a $346 experience, not $346 worth of snacks. And suddenly we

A

were directly under the Statue of Liberty. After struggling for a few minutes to take selfies in which she was visible through the boat windows, almost everyone abandoned their pet-rock champagne glasses and raced out to the deck.

"That was the opposite of worth it," one well-dressed man grumbled to his date while we were on our way out there and he was on his way back in. Don't say that to your Valentine! It was very cold, and Lizzie and I were drunk. I couldn't hold my pen to write in my tiny Atlantic notebook with its tiny cartoon Poseidon on the front. "There's our captain," Lizzie said, pointing up at the captain in his little room above our heads. "The water looks nice," she said, pointing down at the black waves. It was really too dark for pictures.

LIZZIE: These are the kinds of conversation starters I'm bringing to the table. You can't teach that kind of stuff.

Back inside, we wondered how we were going to fit two more glasses of champagne into the remaining 20 minutes of the ride. It turns out, we weren't really. Our final glass—a Lambrusco, which we were told pairs well with "rich Italian dishes" and "dark-chocolate ganache"—was poured right before docking. By the time I came back from a trip to the WC (also airplane-like), we were already being encouraged to depart the vessel, and I hadn't even had a sip of the 'brusco.

KAITLYN: The couple across the plexiglass from us were really in distress because they had paid the optional $50 or something for a whole special bottle of champagne in addition to the four glasses per person that everyone was served in what turned out to be less than one hour. They were not going to have time to drink it. "Chug," the boy said to his date. They chugged. They didn't finish. They put on their coats. He said, not meanly but not nicely, "Never ask me how much this cost." I thought she could easily find out how much it cost without asking him, but I didn't say anything.

I was busy listening to Liza Minnelli's version of "New York, New York," which was playing over the sound system. It was our cue—Get off the boat because there is another group of people waiting to get on. Oh, and my eyes just filled with tears!

After we debarked, we leaped over the rats on 22nd Street (I screamed and Lizzie said, "What a shriek"), and then we asked ourselves: Was ours the longest relationship present on the 7:15 Champagne Tasting Cruise around New York Harbor? And, not to be rude, maybe the only one that will "go the distance"? It absolutely had to be, if only because everyone else was so, so young.

LIZZIE: Inspired by Kaitlyn, I kept an eye out for the magic of Val Day on my way home. At West Fourth, there was a fight on the subway platform: two men screaming at each other. At Fulton, our conductor announced that we should "consider taking another train because . . . uhhh . . . we're not moving." I saw only two people with flowers, but they did look happy to have them.

Later, I couldn't get my contact out of my right eye. I kept squishing around in there until my eye was a Valentine's Day shade of pink. Eventually, I noticed the contact sitting in the sink, where I guess it landed after I'd pried it out without realizing it. I think Valentine's Day is kind of like that: prodding yourself in the eyeball until it hurts a little bit, looking for clarity that you'll probably end up finding somewhere else entirely.

# CELEBRATING 4/20 WHEN
# YOU HATE BEING HIGH

*April 2022*

KAITLYN: I really hesitate to talk about weed on the internet. If I say I love the stuff, there are many who will mock me: *Oh, you're so COOL; you're into DRUGS*. If I say I hate it and have often wept because it makes me feel so bad, there are many who will mock me: *nerd, cop*. Well, these are the risks we take when we are being honest. I really do not like weed.

Until this past week, Lizzie and I had never celebrated 4/20 together before, for the simple reason that I had never celebrated 4/20 with anyone because I famously do not like being high. Regardless, we decided this would be the year to do it, because, first of all, weed is now legal in New York State, which eliminates some of the stress of procuring it, wandering around with it, talking about it on the internet, etc. (Not to say that I'm such a loser that I would have been really, really nervous before . . .) Second, the pandemic reportedly "created a new generation of stoners," including our friend Claire, who pivoted her Finstagram to stoner comedy for parts of 2020 and recently wrote a moving essay about hiding weed from her landlord. It seemed like it might be fun to celebrate if we did it with her, and if we made it into a whole thing. Also, I'm always wondering if basic facts of my personality and body might turn out to be figments of my imagination and therefore possible to randomly alter. If I tried weed just one more time, with Lizzie, on a holiday, would I love it?

LIZZIE: I don't think that "celebrating 4/20" is something anyone really does, except maybe brands, but we have a newsletter to write and we needed a theme. The first time I smoked weed was in junior high; we walked to some abandoned train tracks in our town and smoked out of a Coke can. Then we watched *Clerks*. Classic stuff! Later, my parents would grow weed behind our garage and use it as a stocking stuffer. This is all to say that now I feel about weed the same way I feel about, like, Ritz crackers: There's probably a stale pouch around somewhere, it doesn't matter if you have some or not, and no one should go to jail for it.

We were planning to eat and/or smoke weed for the purposes of this newsletter that you're reading, and also because we were going to Brooklyn Hots, a recently opened BYOB restaurant in Clinton Hill that serves "garbage plates." The garbage plate is a dish that originated in Kaitlyn's birthplace of Rochester, New York, and consists of several food items (hot dogs, hamburgers, macaroni salad, baked beans, home fries, "meat sauce") composed into a single wet, edible mound. Kind of a stoner's smorgasbord.

KAITLYN: To be clear, I was nervous about the weed and about the garbage plates—especially together. Are hometown nostalgia and mind-altering substances typically a great mix?

At 6 p.m. on 4/20, I walked to Lizzie's apartment and she presented me with her "stash." She had a pre-rolled joint we decided to take with us to dinner. She had two packs of gummies (pineapple flavor, raspberry-sorbet flavor) that we didn't dare touch at all because each gummy contained 50 mg of THC. She didn't know why those had been invented or why she was in possession of them. She also had a chic little canister of lime and lemon 10 mg gummies, and we opted to split just one of those before leaving the house.

LIZZIE: We were getting a base high, if you will. Not much happened between my apartment and Brooklyn Hots. On the walk there, we talked about weddings, because it's wedding season and everyone is getting married. We of course said only nice things about the potential shelf life and happiness of those relationships. At some point, Kaitlyn felt lost even though we had basically walked in a straight line for 20 minutes. Maybe this should've been the first indication that the night wasn't going to be a smooth one for her.

KAITLYN: At Brooklyn Hots' companion wine store, I marched in and demanded to know where they shelved the Finger Lakes wines. I have to admit I was not asking in good faith. My suspicion was that, despite being a wine store attached to a Western New York–themed hot-dog restaurant, this store—like, tragically, all wine stores in Brooklyn—would not have many Finger Lakes wines to choose from. Well, I wasn't being nice but I was right, and the clerk said there were actually no Finger Lakes wines in stock at the moment. Mysteriously, seconds later, Lizzie found one anyway. It was from a family winery on Seneca Lake and it was a sparkling blend of several grapes that the Finger Lakes region is known for, not to be annoying— Riesling, Blaufränkisch, Gewürztraminer, Pinot Noir. It was called "Brian's Bright Idea."

While we waited for Claire, we stood underneath the awning of a hideous new apartment building and took turns taking little puffs of the joint. It did not take me long to get to the point of not wanting any more, due to fear.

LIZZIE: We had about 20 minutes to kill, because Claire was coming from a Pure Barre class and you can never tell how long those barre instructors are gonna keep you in there plié-ing for. The building next to us really was quite ugly—sort of a cross between a motel and a prison—and every now and then one of its inhabitants would walk up the outdoor stairs and stare down at us as we tried to light our Massachusetts dispensary joint with some old KGB Bar matches.

Claire showed up wearing a red sweatshirt from Opening Ceremony that had another tiny red sweatshirt sewn onto it. This sweatshirt sweatshirt was a sort of design homage to a denim "pants jacket" with a similar clothing-on-clothing composition that Claire has been hunting for for years. Claire apologized profusely for the Pure Barre–induced delay, but no need: A table was still open inside Brooklyn Hots, waiting for us.

KAITLYN: The interior of Brooklyn Hots was cozy and familiar, with romantic lighting and lots of those metal-and-fiberboard stools from art class. As we looked over the menu, I felt obligated to explain the difference between a "white hot" and a "red hot." The problem was that I didn't know the difference—all I knew was that, during my childhood, at any backyard party or high school soccer game, I would approach the grill and be asked, "Red or white?" And because I like both red hot dogs and white hot dogs, I would answer depending on my mood.

"White hots are . . . sweeter?" I offered. Horribly, we ended up having to ask our waitress for help. (A white hot dog has veal in it and the meat is not cured or smoked; a red hot dog does not typically have veal in it and the meat is cured and smoked.) Embarrassed and high, I then hurried to share all of my other information about Rochester's incredible hot dogs and its famous garbage plates. For example, when President Obama came to Rochester, in 2013, there was local uproar because he did not go to Nick Tahou's, home of the original garbage plate, which is located near the bus station, aka not the most beautiful part of town; instead, he ate half of a grilled-cheese sandwich and some soup at a boring café on Rochester's Park Avenue. (People were right to be mad.) Not long after that, when my college boyfriend came to town, he sampled a garbage plate and later asked to be driven to the hospital, thinking he had appendicitis. Instead I drove him to the house of my aunt who is a nurse and she determined the problem to be gas. (I wish him well.) I should note that, though I have no shame about my heritage, I feel it is obvious why Western New York food culture has not previously been exported.

Brooklyn Hots offered the option of swapping in broccolini for one of the traditional brown or off-white components, which Claire and I both did, for color. The garbage plates there were called "trash plates" because of copyright, and they cost $28.

LIZZIE: I ordered the red and the white hot with macaroni salad and fries. If you're thinking *That doesn't sound like* *something that should be $28,* I don't disagree with you. The servings were huge though, in kind of an unmanageable way. The mass of food went right up to the edge of the plate and had an impressive height of about two inches. Any structural integrity in the dish came solely from the french fries, so it was impossible to move anything around without risking toppling the whole thing.

The last time we had garbage plates together was two summers ago at the aforementioned Nick Tahou's in Rochester, during a week-long vacation in Kaitlyn's home territory. We opened the hatchback of Ashley's Honda Fit and tried to use it as both a table and chairs as we ate in the 90-degree parking lot. No offense to Nick, but those garbage plates were essentially tasteless. The Brooklyn Hots version may have tasted slightly better, but again they were $28 and lukewarm, even though our table was maybe 10 feet from the kitchen.

KAITLYN: It was the honor of my life to take Lizzie and Ashley to the Nick Tahou's parking lot! (Obviously there were limited options for fun during those early months of the pandemic.) They did not need medical care after their first garbage plates, but I think we did all take naps.

If you've almost forgotten about the 4/20 element of this evening, let me assure you that I never did. At all times, I was aware that I had no control over my body and was acting like a freak. I tried to execute a simple iMessage

A

exchange with Nathan and realized I sounded high. I tried to cut my white hot into smaller pieces with the side of my fork and realized I looked high. I tried to explain to Claire that Lizzie was misunderstanding something she was saying because she was using a confusing double negative and realized I was totally high.

At some point, we started talking about the bar in Manhattan where all the bartenders dress as monks. Claire said, erroneously (sorry, Claire), that it was "abbey-themed." Surprisingly, Lizzie then said "abby normal," and I laughed so hard. She was doing *Young Frankenstein*. Claire had never seen it, so Lizzie and I tried to fill her in. I realized I sounded *so* high. I would pause and then try again to speak normally, but then I would only sound even higher than before. I wanted to cry. Claire was like, "I thought you were talking about Classically Abby," which is the influencer moniker of Abigail Roth, sister to nightmare Ben Shapiro. Again I laughed too hard. I tried to concentrate. I took out my phone and typed into the notes app, "abbey, abby, Abby." Then I became obsessed with getting the hell out of Brooklyn Hots, and public, as soon as possible.

LIZZIE: We had fun with abby and fun with niche: Is it pronounced "niche" like "Niche Tahou's" or "niche" like "niches and nephews"? Do you know what I mean? It really was time to leave though, because Kaitlyn was rapidly losing touch with reality and because we had been there for almost an hour and a half.

I was going to suggest that Kait and I split a car home, because I live on the way to where she lives. But before I knew it she was gone, ducking swiftly and soundlessly into an Uber like a celebrity trying to weather a scandal. Five minutes later she texted me and Claire, "Wait I'm so stupid, my car just passed Lizzie's house." Claire also tried to put me in her car, but her app was malfunctioning. It's not like I couldn't find my own way home though, and I did.

KAITLYN: From the Uber, I texted Claire and Lizzie that I was high and unhappy and that I didn't think I would ever want to go back to Brooklyn Hots. I was struggling. I really got to a dark place. . . . And I'm going to share what honestly went through my mind.

The night before, I had rewatched the episode of *The Sopranos* in which mob boss Tony Soprano and his terrifying subordinate Paulie Walnuts have to lam it to Miami because New Jersey is hot with the possibility of murder charges. At the midpoint of their road trip, they stop at a Virginia hotel and enter with visions of room-service steak and cocktails like they'd had during the criminal misadventures of years past, but are informed that the hotel can provide only "cold wraps and salads." Their faces go slack. They are amazed. This is not the way the world should be, and it is unbelievable. Even knowing what we know about Tony and Paulie—the state of their souls, the things they've done, how much they've mercilessly extracted from God's creation—a viewer can't help but agree. Cold wraps and salads? Have you ever heard four words so awful? The situation is probably thanks to global capitalism, somehow, or maybe life just gets worse as we get older and that's all it does. High, looking at my receipt from Brooklyn Hots, I felt that I was having the same experience, albeit separated by space and time and the barrier between fiction and reality. Even knowing the state of my soul, the things I've done, how much I've mercilessly extracted from God's creation, can it really be true that I must now pay $36, including tax and tip, for hot dogs? I got so sad. When I was a child I never had to think about where my next hot dog was coming from. Hot dogs were just around, like corn fields or roads. "Red or white?"

*I should be grateful that there are hot dogs in the world at all,* I told myself. *I should give thanks that I still have half of a hot dog for later, wrapped up in my tote bag.* But I couldn't. I was too sad. I really hate weed and as you can see, it is not for me.

LIZZIE: Me? I drank an orange tea and went to bed, thinking, *What will we write about? Did anything even happen?*

# HOW TO PIVOT ON A
# THURSDAY NIGHT

_____

*July 2022*

LIZZIE: It's getting hot out there, huh? The weather, the housing market, the trend of eating eggplant parm while wearing a claw clip. Everything costs $32, my lease is up in two weeks, and my landlord won't respond to any texts or emails. Better get out and let off some steam before we boil over.

Cut to: a recent Thursday night, looking for something to do. Maybe a potentially unsettling eat-while-singing restaurant in Williamsburg? A poker night? A play we've been thinking about buying tickets for, but haven't bought tickets for? Any of these things could potentially be newsletter-worthy; the problem is, you never know until you go.

We landed on going to the opening night of *The Patriot*, a group art show at O'Flaherty's on Avenue C. The gallery had posted an open call in June allowing anyone to show work, provided they could get it to the gallery somehow. ("If it can hang on the wall, we will show it.") Apparently hundreds of people had submitted work, and now we had the chance to see it, if we could just get inside the building.

KAITLYN: It sure is steaming. My air conditioner is leaking onto the floor as I write this—my super will deal with it as soon as he is done taking several phone calls inside my closet. I have a peeling sunburn on exactly one-half of my body—split vertically, like a Trix yogurt, the product of a beach-umbrella-geometry miscalculation.

We've been moving slowly this month: a week at the lake; a day at the beach; a dinner by the water with Ashley, queen of Greek cuisine. Over beers and saganaki, we talked about how we had missed the *Shrek* rave, how the shoreline itself isn't eventful enough to describe, and how the "Calamari & Comedy" shows at Randazzo's Clam Bar don't start until 11 p.m. How would we, through our sleepiness, be able to communicate to our readers just how fun and outgoing we really still are? Luckily, we're on social media . . . so we saw a few posts about *The Patriot*, the so-called event of the summer. Also, my high school friend Christina was in town. She'd gone to art school, so she would be able to lend a professional eye.

Christina's expertise actually came in handy before we even arrived at the show, as she assured me on the subway that there was no way we could be the least cool women there. If the Ohio art world (she lives in Columbus) is full of posturing people without a clue, she reasoned, the New York art world could be only more posturing and less clued-in. I didn't grasp this logic in the traditional sense, but I did cling to it like a talisman the rest of the way to Manhattan.

After a sweaty jog into CVS to buy Christina a claw clip—we had to get her hair off of her neck!—and then past the dumpling-and-weed-gummy proprietors of St. Mark's Place, we met Lizzie and Matt at Holiday Cocktail Lounge for a quick pregame and a round of snacks. I had two pineapple daiquiris and five mushroom pierogies, while Christina had one multicolored cocktail with a plastic dinosaur in it and a giant pretzel with a large spot of mossy green mold. When she came back from the bathroom, she whispered to me that her claw clip had fallen out of her hair and into the toilet. When Lizzie came back from the bathroom, she whispered to me with a nervous look: "There was a claw clip in my toilet."

Christina said if the art show was a dud we could shave her head for content.

LIZZIE: It was nice of her to offer!

By the time we made it to Avenue C, it was about 8:45, which apparently was not nearly early enough. We walked into a mass of people standing around outside the gallery and Christina asked the crowd, "Is this where the art is?" One guy told us that the line to get in was around the corner, but that he had already given up on it. We turned the corner and walked past hundreds of people (maybe more?), and just as we made it to the end of the line, tired and gasping for water, the cops pulled up with their flashing lights on. It was kind of a lost cause for us after that.

Apparently there's a pillow in there which may or may not be "on loan from The Morgan Library." The Morgan Library! Nothing could be funnier. We're planning to go back at some point, on a less event-of-the-season kind of night.

KAITLYN: I also find it very funny that someone at the show was reportedly telling people that the pillow was specifically "Lincoln's death pillow," but because *The Atlantic* is a facts-oriented institution, I feel like I should point out that the real Lincoln death pillow is on display at the scene of the crime, in Washington, DC. The blood-stained flag that Lincoln's head was wrapped up in is held elsewhere, but it was loaned to my hometown's historical society for no apparent reason in 2008. We had a parade with a Lincoln impersonator and everything. This was a different time in American life. If someone suggested that event today, there would undoubtedly be some faction of the population who would challenge the idea on the grounds that mentioning the outcome of the Civil War constitutes critical race theory.

Anyway, speaking of patriotism—back to *The Patriot*. As Lizzie mentioned, there were hundreds or thousands of people in the street. "I guess the line kind of is the party," they were telling one another. "This is part of the true experience, I think," someone offered. I admit I didn't want to stay, but I understood what was seductive about an opportunity to be out on a summer night holding an open container and looking around at half of the hot 24-year-olds in America, plus a professional contortionist, two email-newsletter reporters, and Juiceboxxx, a musician that Lizzie likes. I caught the energy for five minutes. I heard someone say "iconic," and I thought, *Could be!* I turned to see some downtown boy who is famous on Instagram and who was dressed like James Spader in *Pretty in Pink*—I shrieked against my will. Then I laughed to cover it up. When the cops came, Matt was calm. "Art is now illegal," he told us.

We didn't leave because of the police presence, though. We left because, as we said, there was no way we were getting to the art. I became frantic about the evening turning into a disappointment and texted Stephanie, "*Famous People* emergency!" Minutes later, a black Suburban whisked us away to brownstone Brooklyn. We were headed to Branded Saloon, where Stephanie has attended a karaoke night almost every Thursday for the entire time I've known her. Part two!

LIZZIE: If there's anything people working in marketing will tell you, it's that you have to be ready to pivot at any time. So karaoke it was! I hadn't been to this karaoke night before, despite its somewhat legendary reputation in the friend group, because I tend to avoid activities that require public singing.

I'll preempt any anticipation now; I didn't sing. I'm sorry! I know the point of karaoke is singing.

It's like going to an amusement park and not riding any rides. But the problem is I can't sing. Anytime I say that, people are like, "Oh, that doesn't matter." And for most of the population, it doesn't. But the truth is that nothing I can do even comes close to singing. I have enough trouble pronouncing vowels in a normal way. I literally think it's kind of hard to say my full name. My tongue always feels too big for my mouth when I say it. I can't sing!

It's not like I have zero karaoke experience. I've been known to do an uncomfortably sad Daniel Johnston song if that's on the menu, but usually it's not. When I volunteered at Bonnaroo one year in college, I was stationed at the Garnier Fructis salon, where there was also a karaoke stage. In exchange for a festival pass and a meal token, I had to spend hours applying Garnier Fructis–branded temporary tattoos onto the body of any salon-goer who wanted one, generally wherever they wanted it applied (usually shirtless men, usually on their chests). And the only distraction from my nipple-tattoo apprenticeship was watching the people who had decided to do karaoke at the Garnier Fructis salon during a music festival. One woman wanted to sing "Rehab," but the Garnier Fructis salon didn't have that song, so, undeterred, she sang it acapella. You can see how I've been burned before.

KAITLYN: I badly wanted Lizzie to sing, but I understand that you can't just berate someone into doing a "fun" activity in public. (We learned this from the episode of *Vanderpump Rules* in which Stassi almost breaks up with her boyfriend because he pressures her to dance on a bar even after she explains that she's wearing Spanx under her dress and doesn't feel sexy.)

Branded Saloon is an unassuming but not underground institution. Stephanie recently saw Kid Cudi there, and I believe the place has appeared in a *New York Magazine* spread or two. On this night, when we arrived, there was almost nobody in the vaguely antler-themed back room. This was odd because Stephanie was just about to do "Don't Rain on My Parade," which she absolutely killed, and you would think they could have been selling tickets. Speaking again of patriots, she was wearing jean shorts and a red T-shirt and red lipstick and drinking a Bud Light—I must have taken 400 photos. Later she did "Only the Good Die Young," with a little preamble about

A

her identity as a Catholic. I took a video of that and put it on my Instagram Story, captioned, "Not in a trad way!"

At some point after that, I wrote down in my iPhone notes: "All girls are carrying around the free VOTE NYC pens." Supposedly this is something I observed. By that point, the room was filling up and I'd had a couple of rum and Diet Cokes, bracing myself to take the stage.

LIZZIE: I think karaoke requires you to be pretty vulnerable, because if there are a lot of unexpected oohs in your song choice, or lengthy instrumental breaks that you forgot about, or if you sing, for example, the Red Hot Chili Peppers, but realize mid-song that you can't quite match the cocaine cadence of Anthony Kiedis (few can!), you need the crowd to go along with you for the ride anyway. You can't get off the Scrambler just because you feel like you might barf.

But the group at Branded Saloon defied karaoke expectations. There were some impressive singers, as there almost always are at these places, but no hierarchy. It was kind of like, as soon as you got behind the mic, the crowd became your parents and they were proud of you no matter what. It wasn't hard to understand why people go there every week.

I hesitate to even mention this other thing, but I will for the sake of transparency. When Matt took the stage to sing "Dreams" by the Cranberries, someone, a confident and vocally blessed opera-type singer, probably one of the best singers in the room, sang along loudly enough to totally drown out Matt, even though he had a microphone. Matt was kind of salty after that, because no one could hear his Irish accent. Stephanie confirmed that it was not good "karaoke etiquette" to sing louder than the song-picker. Them's the breaks!

KAITLYN: Lizzie's right; that stank. I tried to make a big show of putting my hand behind my ear and inclining my body toward the stage, to indicate that I could not hear the person who was standing on it, but to no avail. I guess this is how a great rivalry is born . . .

As a group, we got a lot of singing in, even though you couldn't hear all of it all of the time. Christina did Paramore because we went to Warped Tour together as children. She got the crowd on their feet and screaming for "That's What You Get," a song that reverberates in my bones because of how many times I blasted it in my grandma's Chevy Malibu on my way to work at the mall. Stephanie did Jo Dee Messina's "Heads Carolina, Tails California," literally the best song ever written or performed, also for me. How did this become about me? I don't know, but I loved it! I sang "Boys of Summer" and then "Mama's Broken Heart." Those are my two karaoke songs.

LIZZIE: Here's where we say something about finding art in unexpected places—just kidding! The truth is, karaoke was fun and there were no cops there. That's all we really wanted. Plus it's almost better that we couldn't get into *The Patriot*. For the story!

KAITLYN: I was proud of us because we executed a pivot and survived flagging energy to "make a night of it"— that's called New York acrobatics. We even closed the place down: Stephanie and Christina and I went up together for the final song, Faith Hill's (actually iconic) "This Kiss." I was really pleased that the karaoke DJ, Jared, gave us this spot of honor in the lineup. He does choose, you know.

I guess I was dizzier and drunker than I thought during the back half of the night, because almost none of the notes I took for this newsletter made any sense. The last one was "Biden '24." I truly can't imagine why I would have written that.

## ABOUT THE AUTHORS

KAITLYN TIFFANY is a staff writer at *The Atlantic*. She writes about online platforms and internet culture. She is the author of the book *Everything I Need I Get from You: How Fangirls Created the Internet as We Know It*.

LIZZIE PLAUGIC is a creative strategist and writer. Previously, she was a reporter at *The Verge*, where she wrote about internet culture.